ENDORSEMENTS FOR

HOW COMPANIES WIN

"The lessons of yesterday will not pave a path to the future. Those who adapt to and understand the new rules and the new models will ultimately win. The authors underscore the need to look at the world and its changing dynamics in a whole new way."
—AJAY BANGA, PRESIDENT AND CEO MASTERCARD

"With all of the options shoppers have today, it's critically important to understand demand. It's how you satisfy your customers better than your competitors. It's the way companies will win."
—BRIAN CORNELL, PRESIDENT AND CEO, SAM'S CLUB

"How Companies Win shows how to successfully manage in the future. Its fresh look at data and the case histories will stimulate the imagination of every business leader."
—MARY DILLON, PRESIDENT AND CEO, U.S. CELLULAR

"The authors got it right. Profitable growth is the real driver of value creation. Showing how companies can grow is the book's real contribution."
—JIM JENNESS, CHAIRMAN AND FORMER CEO
OF THE KELLOGG COMPANY

"Calhoun and Kash have taken on the biggest business question of all: what it will take for companies to win in this new era of growing oversupply and heightened global competition. The conclusions they reach are eye-opening. And they serve as a warning that every executive—and every investor—should shift their focus to the demand chain right now or risk losing their competitive edge."
—HENRY R. KRAVIS, COFOUNDER OF
KOHLBERG KRAVIS ROBERTS & CO.

"As consumer behaviors change more quickly all the time, demand must be analyzed in greater depth than ever before. Understanding how media companies, retailers, and manufacturers work together to serve demand with much greater precision will be key to the success of all companies going forward."
—LESLIE MOONVES, PRESIDENT AND CHIEF EXECUTIVE OFFICER
OF CBS CORPORATION

"The rise of social networks has amplified the individual's voice and this has sparked a revolution in demand. How Companies Win *offers real-world solutions that you can implement right now to take advantage of these changes."*

—SHERYL SANDBERG, COO, FACEBOOK

"The authors' discussion of Precision as the 5th P adds a powerful new tool for marketers. It aligns exactly with our strategy of precision marketing."

—JOSEPH TRIPODI, CHIEF MARKETING AND COMMERCIAL OFFICER, COCA-COLA COMPANY

"A persuasive case that winning in today's market requires an understanding that supply-driven business models of the past will not keep pace with fundamental changes in our global economy and its digitally enabled consumer."

—JACK WELCH

HOW COMPANIES WIN

Also by Rick Kash

The New Law of Demand and Supply

HOW
COMPANIES
WIN

PROFITING FROM DEMAND-DRIVEN BUSINESS MODELS
NO MATTER WHAT BUSINESS YOU'RE IN

RICK KASH and **DAVID CALHOUN**

HARPER
BUSINESS

An Imprint of HarperCollins*Publishers*
www.harpercollins.com

HarperCollins books may be purchased for educational, business, or sales promotional use. For information, please write: Special Markets Department, HarperCollins Publishers, 10 East 53rd Street, New York, NY 10022.

Designed by Level C

Library of Congress Cataloging-in-Publication Data
Kash, Rick
How companies win : profiting from demand-driven business models no matter what business you're in / Rick Kash, David Calhoun.–1st ed.
p. cm.
ISBN 978-0-06-200045-3 (hardback)
1. Organizational change. 2. Organizational effectiveness 3. Customer relations
4. Customer satisfaction 5. Customer services—Management 6. Success in Business.
I. Calhoun, David. II. Title.
HD58. 8 .K3767 2010
658.4'012—dc22
2010024371

10 11 12 13 14   OV/RRD   10 9 8 7 6 5 4 3

CONTENTS

PART III
EXECUTION

       Aligning Your Company for Success

EIGHT **The Demand Chain**   195
       Collaborative Networks Power a Profit Search Engine

NINE   **Supply, Meet Demand**   209
       The Partnership of Supply and Demand

AFTERWORD **A Fresh Start**   223

       Notes   233
       Index   243

ACKNOWLEDGMENTS

A book like this one is always a collaboration of more than just the authors. Dozens of people, working each day on the front lines of real-life business, finding pragmatic solutions as they go, have made this book possible. They have guided our thinking, our beliefs, and our views on how companies will win today and in the future. We thank them all.

However, there are a few people without whose contributions the book would not have been possible—and we'd like to single them out for special recognition and gratitude.

To Jason Green, who has been our partner in this endeavor, we are grateful for the quality of his thinking, his candor, and his tireless devotion to making every part of this book better. No one could wish for, or benefit from, a better partner. This book is yours as much as it is ours.

It takes a professional at the highest ranks of the economic discipline to align Adam Smith's thinking to the reality of today's economy. Dr. Venkatesh Bala is the Chief Economist of The Cambridge Group. He first identified the demand economy and has provided the foundation for establishing the primacy of demand in a world which faces continuous oversupply.

If you write a book, Jim Levine should be your literary agent. It's really just that simple. He's a great representative, and an even better coach and friend.

Hollis Heimbouch, publisher of the Harper Business imprint of HarperCollins, has believed in our vision for the future of business from day one. Once the work began, however, she completely fulfilled her mission to clarify what we should communicate with our readers. There is an old expression which says, "If two people always agree, then one of them is unnecessary." Hollis has been very, very necessary. Thanks also to Matt Inman who works so closely with Hollis.

"Ghost Writer" has always seemed a strange term, but never more so than when you work with our writing partner, Michael S. Malone. He has written in our voice, but his own voice has seamlessly melded with ours. His broad experience in business, and depth of knowledge about Silicon Valley and the digital world has enriched our story. We asked a lot of Mike, but he gave us much more than we asked for.

Gloria Cox is the Managing Partner of The Cambridge Group. She has magically balanced her large family and professional career while simultaneously earning her master's degree in Divinity, with distinction, from the McCormick Theological Seminary. She has helped in all phases of the book and her leadership has made it possible for us to complete this project.

Dr. Kevin Bowen has been Rick's business partner for twenty-five years. Much of the intellectual capital contained in these pages is the result of Kevin's singular talents.

A book is made up of seemingly endless details and the constant requirement for accuracy. It takes a unique person to keep everything moving forward. For our book, Linda Deeken is that person.

Mark Henneman has taken the strategy and the concept of the demand chain, which we introduce in this book, and turned it into reality. He will greatly influence the business model advocated in this book in order to help companies win in the demand economy.

To make the demand chain practical and actionable, we also wish to thank Dr. Louise Keely, Mary Blue, and many others in The Nielsen Company and The Cambridge Group.

To Eddie Yoon, whose energy and enthusiasm is contagious, thanks for helping us shape this book and its content.

As you'll read in this book, we believe the demand-led supply chain is the new business model for success in the twenty-first century. Steve Matthesen and Paul Upchurch of Nielsen have played a significant role in furthering this concept and in architecting the key building blocks to bring it to life.

John Lewis, Mark Leiter, Steve Hasker, Jim Cuminale, Itzhak Fisher, and Tim Murray are all senior executives at Nielsen. They have constructively challenged our thinking and in every case improved our output. As they traveled around the world, they were always available, and always generous with their time.

We wanted a call to action for our readers so they can take what we've written in our book and apply the principles to how they manage their companies. There can be no more compelling call to action than the successful growth stories we recount throughout this book.

The business cases you will read are the success stories that were led by, and inspired by, a group of business leaders. They have worked with us so that the story of their companies could be told. In each and every case, these leaders have selflessly shared their business strategies, how they have engaged their organizations, and the paths they have taken in order to grow their companies and their brands.

This distinguished group includes Jim Kilts, Dave West, J. P. Bilbrey, Tom Wilson, Barry Judge, Dave Peacock, Keith Levy, Ed Liddy, C. J. Fraleigh, Philippe Schaillee, Rick Lenny, Jim Skinner, and Steve Hughes. On a personal basis, every one of them has enthusiastically participated beyond our greatest expectations. Ultimately, this is their story. Individually and collectively they have our admiration and our gratitude.

Stacey Gallagher and Deborah Dean: only the four of us can fully understand the enormous [both personal and professional] contributions you have made to this book.

To our readers, we hope that you will benefit from *How Companies Win*. If we are successful in influencing your thinking, then our purpose will have been served.

HOW COMPANIES WIN

INTRODUCTION

A NEW STRATEGY FOR A NEW ERA

Why did venerable car insurance giant Allstate start offering more features and customer choices that went against conventional risk practices?

How did Best Buy manage to thrive even as its biggest competitor, Circuit City, went out of business?

How did Ball Park Franks, which its parent company Sara Lee was considering deemphasizing in 2005, become one of the nation's hottest consumer brands just two years later?

How did Bud Light Lime become one of the fastest-growing new beer introductions in the last thirty years?

What gave the CEO of Hershey's the confidence to share his competitive strategy with the entire food industry?

The answers to these questions reflect a fundamental shift in the relationship between supply and demand in the global economy. It is a shift from a supply-driven economy to a demand-driven economy. It is a shift that requires a new set of strategies and tools.

The centuries-old definition of demand is a simple one: quantity sought at a given price. But experience has taught us that demand is much more complex: *Demand is what customers possess in terms of the needs and desires—emotional, psychological, and physical—they want satisfied*, and *have the purchasing power to satisfy*. For companies, demand is ultimately about *profit*. At the end of the day, whoever satisfies demand the best, profits most.

In the pages ahead, we will explain and illustrate the dynamics of demand more thoroughly, all in service of the three goals of this book: 1) to help you understand the forces behind the shift from a supply-driven to a demand-driven economy; 2) to help you develop the business strategies required by that shift; and 3) to provide you with the tools for executing that shift.

Using case studies drawn from our consulting work with clients and other demand-driven companies, we will show you how companies are winning in the demand economy and how you too can win, no matter what sector or part of the world your business operates in.

DISEQUILIBRIUM AND DISINTERMEDIATION

For more than a generation, business has been extraordinarily focused on the supply chain: building it, perfecting it, defending it. And the modern corporation depends on the supply chain to continually generate profits, because organic growth has been so hard to achieve.

The great companies of the past have always taken an historic innovation—AT&T with the telephone, Ford with cars, IBM with computers—and then consolidated control by defending their distribution arm at all costs. But the fastest-growing companies of today, such as Apple, Amazon, Facebook, Twitter, and Google, don't focus nearly as much on distribution channels. Instead, their businesses are built around *consumption* models, and their single-minded focus is on building relationships to their family of consumers to earn their trust, to expand their role in their consumers' lives, and to enlist them in everything from product design to service.

These twenty-first-century enterprises are as focused on constantly improving their levels of trust with their customers and consumers as they are on the degrees of efficiency of supply.

And that is only half of the story. Even as this cultural shift is taking place, the nature of distribution itself is undergoing a transformation. Today, most manufacturing business models are still built around the traditional notion of a physical community of towns and roads, warehouses and delivery trucks, advertising and point-of-sale marketing. Not surprisingly then, most supply chains are also built around local physical stores and factories.

But what happens in a world where one's neighborhood is as much virtual as physical? When your friends and other key influencers are scattered around the world? What happens when a single opinion, via a blog or Web posting, can influence a billion consumers on four continents? For these questions, the traditional supply-centric business model has few answers.

Every great step forward in business history, from the Industrial Revolution to the brand management system to the virtual corporation, has taken place at the system level. That is, how do you coordinate assets, information, and people? Today, the Internet is the ultimate such system, bigger than any that came before. Can we be surprised then that it reverses that most traditional of business relationships, the one between manufacturer and customer? Or that the old supply model is now beginning to seek new solutions in a world in which the consumer, for the first time ever, is enthroned in the driver's seat of the global economy?

We were given an advance warning of this trend more than a decade ago, during the so-called dot-com bubble. Unfortunately, we drew all of the wrong conclusions from that period. Even today, that era, with its creation and destruction of thousands of new companies, is typically seen as an example of wasteful runaway business growth.

To the contrary, we should look back on the dot-com era as being one of extraordinary importance. The "big idea" in the air in the 1990s was *disintermediation:*[1] the notion that business systems, empowered by the new information and communications technologies, would strip out the middleman and grow more efficient in the process. The dot-com era was essentially this idea of disintermediation, propelled by the Internet, reaching the retail world—replacing traditional bricks-and-mortar businesses with e-commerce companies.

As we all know, the explosion of thousands of new online retailers that targeted almost every retail business from overstock inventory to groceries to pet food was followed instead by a massive shakeout in the industry that quickly killed the vast majority[2] of those companies. The dot-com bubble was followed by the dot-com bust.

But on closer inspection, the story is much more interesting. The fact is that almost all of those e-commerce companies were retail-driven enterprises, often driven by old-line supply companies. And if you had looked at their business plans, you would have noticed that few of them had any idea exactly who would buy these products or services (Pets.com being the most notorious example). In fact, very few had any fulfillment capability or competitive advantage to speak of.

By comparison, those companies that did survive the shakeout—Amazon, eBay, Yahoo, Orbitz, Google—have proven to be some of the most important and influential companies of recent years. And they in turn set the pattern for the Web 2.0 social media firms such at Twitter, MySpace, Facebook, and YouTube that have redefined modern life. What did those survivors have in common? Their business was based on what customers wanted, rather than what the suppliers already had. They were the harbingers of the demand-driven economy, if only we had noticed.

One of the lessons they taught is that we have now entered an era of oversupply. Oversupply is a situation where significantly more supply exists than there is demand to absorb it. Oversupply is often characterized by a lack of differentiation, with price becoming the primary factor underlying purchase decisions. As a consequence, pricing power virtually disappears, and organic growth and profitability become increasingly difficult to achieve.

The second lesson to be learned is that in an era of oversupply it is now imperative that you construct a framework in your company that encompasses and aligns everyone toward meeting not just the current but the latent and emerging demand of your highest-profit customers and consumers. And before you can do that, you need to understand who those customers and consumers are, where they are, and what "need states" they exhibit as they make their purchasing decisions. The concept of need states is important for developing an in-depth understanding of demand. Need states are the circumstances or the occasions that cause someone to want something and to take action in its pursuit. Think of how Gatorade invented the need state of the "hot and sweaty" occasion and built its business around knowing more about that need state than any of its competitors.

As we'll show you in this book, the transformation you must make in your company and the reversal you must make in your perspective will be easier than you think. This is not reengineering; this is *rethinking*. This is not reorganizing, it's reshaping manufacturers, retailers, and the media into a collaborative network that will work to the benefit of all who participate. For a long time, this new model of organizing and collaborating has been intuitively felt, and now it's real. It's called the "demand chain." In this book we will demonstrate the growing arsenal of tools you have at your disposal—including new mental models, more precise ways to develop pricing strategy, "demand profit pools," and demand-led supply chains—to find and capture the highest-profit customers and consumers in your market, to find safe harbors of equilibrium in an increasingly distorted global economy, and most of all, to win in the new demand-based economy.

DEFINING DEMAND

Since the time Adam Smith wrote about the notion, economists have sought a succinct way to describe what they mean by demand. Their definition is often as simple as stating that demand is the quantity sought at a given price. We have found the concept of demand to be far more profound, and one that is closely related to, but distinct from, the concept of physiological need.

While need is purely physical in nature, demand includes physical, psychological, and emotive components, backed by economic purchasing power. Demand is both near term and longer term, not just the instantaneous fulfillment of a need.

For example, a person might *need* a glass of water to quench his thirst on a warm day, but he could *demand* much more from a bottle of water. In addition to addressing the body's physiological requirement with the latter, he might care about portability, derive reassurance and pleasure from the knowledge that the water's source is a pure spring nestled deep in the mountains, and appreciate the aesthetic contours of the container in which the water is held.

Step into the minds of people who buy bottled water—and there are many—and you will learn of this multidimensional calculus in their heads as they walk into a store to purchase a bottle. It is why the need for water translates into the multibillion-dollar demand for bottled water, and indeed, it is why, for something so humble and basic, there is such a profusion of sources, shapes, compositions, brands, and— importantly—price points, for what is thought to be, simply a bottle of water. Just so, an enterprise seeking simply to serve the physiological need will get a purchase and not much more, whereas one that understands and properly addresses the demand stands to gain far more in pricing power, undying loyalty, and lifetime value.

Demand is multidimensional in other ways and can also be classified as current, latent, and emerging. To understand the difference between those three types of demand, consider the history of competition for the Internet. In 1995, as the Web was just emerging as a major new consumer market, a small company, Netscape, became a business phenomenon by commercializing a Web browser program originally developed by the University of Illinois Urbana-Champaign under the name Mosaic.[3]

Netscape Navigator, as it was now called, enabled the new generation of Web users to more efficiently "surf" the Web, and it quickly gained millions of users. Microsoft, which was the largest supplier of software to the personal computer industry through such products as the underlying operating system (Microsoft Windows) and professional productivity tools (Microsoft Office, especially Word), was caught napping by this Web browser revolution, and scrambled to respond.

With a vast market already established by Netscape, Microsoft was faced with the challenge of responding to *current* demand. It did so by developing its own similar Web browser, Internet Explorer, and then drove that product into the marketplace by (controversially) embedding it in its already-dominant Windows OS. By 1999, Explorer had surpassed Navigator in users[4]—and by 2002 had reached 95 percent market share.[5]

About the same time that Internet Explorer was overtaking Netscape Navigator, two Stanford graduate students, Sergey Brin and Larry Page,[6] sensed that a growing number of people were sharing their own frustration with searching the rapidly expanding Web for the right Web sites. The solution they developed, which they called "Google," revolutionized the search by looking at total viewers rather than just key words.

Google, as everyone knows, was almost an instant phenomenon, not just because it was free, but because it fulfilled a need that millions of Internet users had but had yet to fully articulate. As such, it was a classic example of *latent* demand: millions of people never knew they wanted Google . . . until they saw it. And then they instantly incorporated it into their daily lives. Google became the first great tech company of the new century, with revenues of nearly $24 billion in 2009.[7]

The Google model of a free service that creates communities of users proved hugely influential with the rise of a new generation of Internet companies—the so-called Web 2.0 social network firms such as MySpace and Facebook—in the years after 2000. One small company created to deliver podcasting services, Odeo, was acquired by Web veterans Jack Dorsey, Biz Stone, and former Google employee Ev Williams through Obvious Corp. in late 2006.[8] One day, finding themselves in a creative slump over new product ideas, the team held a group brainstorming session. What came out of that meeting was an idea for an extremely simple group-messaging service, an idea that Obvious Corp. cofounder Jack Dorsey had been ruminating over for years.[9] They called it Twitter.

Twitter was never really meant to be more than a minor application. Instead it became a worldwide phenomenon, the fastest growing Web site on the Internet. Four *billion* tweets were sent in the first quarter of 2010.[10]

What explains Twitter's success? It was simple and free, for one thing. But even more important, it tapped into a vast reservoir of demand that was just *emerging*: "smart phone" users who had spent the previous decade becoming acculturated to the daily use of e-mails, instant messages, and Facebook chat. Twitter, rather than being a revolutionary idea, was in fact a small and comfortable next step. Its simplicity and limited power (no more than 140 characters) proved to be an advantage rather than a limitation, and millions of users quickly found its use so familiar as to be almost second nature.

THE DEMAND-DRIVEN CORPORATION

In today's global and rapidly changing economy, current demand is an ante to play in the game. Winners have an equally intense focus on latent and emerging demand. To continue to grow in a world of flattening or even shrinking demand, you are going to have to build on one of the most successful strategies of the past—endlessly fine-tuning a supply chain *for its own sake*—and simultaneously shift to guiding and informing that supply chain with a demand chain that constantly monitors the changing demands and need states of your highest-profit customer pools.

That in turn will require leaders to change how they allocate their precious time—and ultimately force organizations to reorient themselves to a single-minded focus on serving the changing needs of those key customers and consumers. In the business to consumer (B2C) world, those *customers* are the wholesalers, distributors, and retailers who make your offers available to the end users . . . the *consumers* who purchase and use them. For business to business (B2B), *customers* will include other businesses that distribute and sell your offers and ultimately the small-, medium-, and large-sized businesses who are the end users of those offers. While this captures the way we will generally use the terms customer and consumer throughout this book, we recognize that these definitions are often interchangeable and are often blurred in the actual marketplace.

Following this premise of focusing on the most profitable customers and consumers to its logical conclusion results in a company that looks like this:

- It has built its delivery network around the Web, not just highways and roads and standard forms of media.

- It has a proprietary framework through which it manages the business that includes an understanding of demand, supply, competition, innovation opportunity, and profitability.

- It understands how demand profit pools of customers and consumers create greater effectiveness in marketing, results in higher profitability, and continuously achieves organic growth.

- It has built an intelligent system that knows where to hunt for the next profit opportunity. The strategy conversation is about how to serve customers and consumers now—and in the future, which enables your company to consistently preempt competition.

- The company and its expanded network of manufacturers, retailers, and media partners (the demand chain) share the same objectives, including winning with the same high-profit customers and consumers. The network members' common task is to collaborate and to share data in order to merge your objectives and outcomes around the common denominator of the customer/consumer and the demand they are seeking to satisfy.

- It holds its marketing and commercial organizations to the same standards that it holds its supply chain management. And just as its supply chain has metrics for everything, so too must that rigor, rhythm, and consequence apply to its new demand chain.

- It recognizes that intellectual obsolescence is even more expensive than physical obsolescence. It treats information with the same sense of urgency that it does physical inventory. The goal is to continually shorten the time it takes to bring good product, service, and marketing ideas to the marketplace.

- Your company will precisely reach your most profitable customers and consumers. You will have more timely and more precise measurement of your advertising on all three screens (TV, Web, and phone). These programs are already in development, so you never again need to take "no" for an answer.

- It recognizes that alignment *across*—not just *along*—supply and demand chains is critical. In your company, the demand chain orients the supply chain, and the supply chain fulfills the demand chain.

- It is an organization that is confident it can achieve on the demand side what it has achieved on the supply side.

HOW YOUR COMPANY WINS

That's probably a very different kind of company from the one you find yourself in today. But if we are going to win in the new demand economy, this is what all of our companies will look like in the very near future. And even after we've made this transformation, we will still have to devote more time and energy than ever to maintaining it, because human beings are complicated and mercurial and a demand chain that is accurate today may be misdirected tomorrow.

We have before us a great opportunity. Supply wildly outpaces demand right now. The global economy has become unbalanced. And we are going to find the path to win in this new environment. We have the chance to carve out high-profit and defensible markets, and enjoy first-mover advantage.

It goes without saying that there's a learning curve attached to change of this scope. But you have a choice: you can tweak your current operations or you can lead your company to a new business model aligned with the times. It will be a discovery process that *every* contemporary CEO and leadership team—not least of all your competitors—must go through. So the sooner you get through it, the bigger your advantage will be. You can't copy discovery; there is no shortcut. Every company is going to have to navigate its way through this process, cutting its own path. This book is the first step in that discovery process.

It has always been true that the biggest success stories emerge from times of change. Where weak leaders see uncertainty, the confident leader—armed with a smart and differentiated strategy—creates new opportunities to win. This is such a time. And the winning companies will be defined by leaders who fully understand that the time for change is now, and that the opportunity to win has never been bigger or better.

In the pages to come, we will introduce our vision of this demand-driven company. It is the product of more than a decade of work since we first identified the demand economy, and it has been tested in the crucible of real-life business in our work with scores of the world's largest companies. We'll offer examples and case studies of some of the most compelling of these stories in the chapters to come.

For now, what is important to understand is that we believe—and we intend to convince you as well—that demand strategy is an idea whose time has come. That it offers a powerful response to the unprecedented new challenge we face in a world of flat to contracting demand. Further, that we believe that the demand chain will take its place and be an equally powerful complement to the supply chain—that, in fact, you can no longer have a truly efficient supply chain without an equally healthy demand chain. And that ultimately, the combination of the demand chain and the supply chain will take a premiere role for how companies win in the twenty-first century.

In addition to proposing a new demand-based business model, we will share with you a whole new palette of demand management tools, such as mental modeling and the "thesis for winning," already being used by some of the world's most admired corporations. With these tools, which interlink along the demand chain, you will be able to harness demand and turn it to your profit.

We hope that at this point we have you intrigued, if perhaps not yet convinced, about the demand chain and its implications for helping you win. Now let's see how it's done. We'll start with one of the first big success stories of the new demand-driven economy: *How did McDonald's, a troubled and aging company just five years ago, manage to find new life, continuous growth—and new profits?*

PART I

SHIFT

ONE

THE DEMAND-DRIVEN COMPANY

How McDonald's Made the Winning Shift

By almost any measure, McDonald's is one of the most successful and influential companies of all time.

But from the mid-1990s until 2002, the company lost its way by choosing to focus almost exclusively on supply—in its case, building ever more restaurants and acquiring other food chains—rather than on what its millions of customers really wanted. It was only when McDonald's went back to paying attention to those customers—what they liked, what they wanted, and what they might like (i.e., current, latent, and emerging demand)—that the company found its way back to success.

The modern McDonald's story traditionally begins in 1955, when franchisee Ray Kroc opened the ninth store of the fifteen-year-old company.[1] McDonald's had already pioneered the idea of "fast food," but it was Kroc who systematized the process and, buying the company, turned it into an international corporation and a global symbol of American culture. Kroc drove McDonald's to greatness with a single-minded focus on what he called "QSCV"—quality, service, cleanliness, and value.

And it worked brilliantly. By the end of the twentieth century, McDonald's was enjoying revenues of almost $15 billion annually from more than 28,000 stores around the world. Net income was nearly $2 billion in 2000.[2]

But the company was already losing its way. Just two years later, in 2002, McDonald's suffered its first quarterly loss since 1954, ending a celebrated half-century of continual growth.[3] And the bad news kept coming: even as profits disappeared and revenues flattened, consumer satisfaction levels fell below that of the company's major competitors. As a further insult, a spate of articles from 1998 to 1999 that eventually became the book *Fast Food Nation* in 2001 singled out McDonald's as contributing to America's health and obesity problems.[4]

The company scrambled to uncover what had gone wrong after so many years of success, and was stunned at what it discovered: in McDonald's headlong rush to become *bigger*, to dominate the global market, it had lost track of its parallel need to also become *better* at understanding consumers' latent and emerging demand.

The failure of this second half of the company's original strategy was everywhere management looked. The company had been opening an average of 2,000 stores per year for a decade,[5] yet all of that expansion was producing no new incremental income growth. This indicated a base of overbuilding—a fact underscored by the growing anger of veteran franchisees, who complained of new stores taking away their business.

The falling consumer satisfaction numbers were particularly galling. McDonald's, after all, had built its success in part on pristine and bright stores staffed by friendly, well-trained employees. Now, consumers were increasingly complaining about dirty stores, unclean bathrooms, and unfriendly, poorly trained employees. Worse, this growing indifference to consumers seemed to rest at the very top of the company: a quick survey of chairman's letters from 1996 to 2000 found just *one* mention of customer service.[6] If senior management didn't care about service, why should the employees behind the counter?

But perhaps the biggest threat McDonald's now faced was coming from outside the company, in the form of a cultural shift, for which the articles, books, and eventual documentaries were merely a more extreme manifestation. Obesity had become a national crisis in the

United States, the baby boomers who had first driven McDonald's success were now becoming senior citizens, and the younger generations were more health conscious, more likely to eat organic foods, and more likely to be vegetarian than any generations before them. Even the federal government was talking about regulating food.

In response, consumers were shifting to competitors such as Subway, which were perceived as being healthier, while others were consciously trying to stay away from fast food restaurants altogether. Unlike the problems of overexpansion and declining quality, this challenge was not something that could be solved by some thoughtful fine-tuning of McDonald's existing business model. McDonald's realized to its dismay that it needed to revisit its *entire* product offering in order to keep up with the changing tastes of the public.

But the company hadn't become the archetypical enterprise of the late twentieth century by being risk averse. Senior management, in surveying the company's problems, realized that they could all be encompassed with a single description: McDonald's had forgotten QSCV. Now it needed to restore that principle, to add a new factor—*F* for improved food offerings—and to update to the twenty-first century the philosophy that had built the company.

And so McDonald's began 2003 embarking on one of the most remarkable restructurings in modern business history. One of the world's most successful and admired companies would realign to the current, latent, and emerging demands of its customers.

RENAISSANCE

As company executives saw it, McDonald's had three major business challenges to address, and it had to deal with them concurrently: overexpansion, declining customer satisfaction, and cultural transformation. To some degree, they were all interconnected, yet each would require a distinct and independent solution.

Overexpansion

The challenge here was not practical, but psychological. McDonald's could solve its self-cannibalization problems (and devote more time and resources to improving employee training) merely by reducing its annual store openings from about 1,000 per year to fewer than 500[7]—which is ultimately what it did. But before that could happen, the company had to abandon its half-century-old mind-set that *success equaled expansion*.

This was an understandable attitude. The previous half-century had been one long race between the major fast food chains to fill the world's available markets with new franchises. Whoever led the race— and McDonald's had always done just that—was winning the game. Rapidly growing franchises was part of how McDonald's saw itself as a business (what we'll be calling its "mental model"); it was embedded into the company's DNA. Now it would have to not just abandon this philosophy, but literally rewire itself.

Cultural Transformation

The critical articles, books, documentaries, and the proposed legislation, threatening as they were, were also bellwethers of a larger shift taking place in society toward healthier and more natural foods, against cheap calories, and against obesity. Leaving aside the possible threat of government regulation, McDonald's still had to face the prospect of consumers turning away from its food offerings to pursue other lifestyles. To keep that from happening, the company needed to follow the culture, offering new and more healthy items on its menu while still retaining those key products, such as the Big Mac, that were synonymous with McDonald's and gave the company its distinct identity.

Customer Satisfaction

Additional benefits of slowing store expansion included improving the declining margins by cutting costs, freeing up capital to improve existing stores, and giving the company more time to focus on raising quality and training current employees.

The first step, McDonald's realized, was to get back to what it did best, and that meant stripping away all of the noncore businesses it had accumulated by acquisitions in recent years—even the hugely successful ones. That meant divesting itself of the Boston Market chain, Chipotle Mexican food, and a host of specialty and experimental restaurants around the world.[8] The new mind-set at McDonald's would henceforth shift from growing through new stores to doing better at existing storefronts.

But what did "doing better" really mean? McDonald's developed a table[9] that showed the components of customer satisfaction and how they related to the company's own values. McDonald's called this its "Plan to Win" and it addressed five components that constituted McDonald's new model for total customer service: people, products, place, price, and promotion:

Let's look at each in turn:

Improve Quality. Here is where McDonald's proposed to deal with both the challenges of changing consumer tastes and of less-than-pristine facilities. For the first, it meant the construction of a new menu, one that retained the most popular traditional items (Big Mac, McNuggets, Quarter Pounder), but also rolled out a whole new family of healthy alternatives including more salads, bottled water, fruits and nuts, and yogurt, all featuring notification of nutritional content for the health conscious. These healthy items would be matched by the addition to the menu of premium items not traditionally connected with McDonald's: Angus burgers, specialty coffees, snack wraps. The aging facilities would undergo renovation to a new interior look that

Improve Quality	Improve Service	Improve Cleanliness	Improve Value	Augment with Improved Marketing
➢ New menu, including healthier (also perceived as higher quality) items of salads, yogurts, bottled water, fruits, chicken – Nutrition information provided ➢ Newly re-designed store interiors with clean, modern lines and colors	➢ Expand 24-hour service offering ➢ Improve employee training ➢ Eliminate "Made for You" to increase consistency and decrease wait times ➢ Expand menu items to encourage existing customers to come back more regularly	➢ New systems/handheld devices to ensure regular facility cleaning in general and of cooking surfaces/equipment ➢ Newly re-designed store interiors with clean, modern lines give perception of cleanliness ➢ Upgrade restrooms	➢ Broaden menu with new products at low- & high-end price points to create perception of value – Low end customers value $1 menu deals – Higher end customers perceive "pricier" health items a good value ➢ Average sale went from $5 to $12	➢ Support other changes with launch of "i'm lovin' it" campaign ➢ Fundamental idea was of being forever young and McDonald's being customer's favorite place and way to eat ➢ Manifestation of McDonald's renewed focus on customers

Source: McDonald's Annual Reports, secondary literature search.

featured simpler, more contemporary lines and colors. The cost would be covered by some of the money saved by not opening thousands of new stores.

Improve Service. McDonald's also knew that nice stores and an expanded menu wouldn't be enough if consumers found themselves with endless waits and dealing with surly or inept counter and window personnel. The company realized that by scaling back expansion and transforming its offerings, it now had the time and the incentive to focus on recreating the legendary McDonald's service quality, configured for the twenty-first century. The timing would be perfect, too: with focus, the new menu would convince existing customers to stop by McDonald's more frequently—and perhaps lure lost customers back to give the restaurants another try—and the improved ambience, service, and food would capture them. One key to this plan was to use the ramp-up period for additional employee training. Another was to extend hours of service to twenty-four hours in as many restaurants as possible. Finally—and this too was hard to accept, given rival Burger King's success with "Have It Your Way"—McDonald's concluded that eliminating its "Made for You" program would increase consistency (and thus quality) and reduce wait times.

Improve Cleanliness. McDonald's realized that the facilities renovation would go a long way toward improving consumer perception of the cleanliness of its restaurants. But it didn't want to stop there. The bathrooms too needed renovation and upgrading, both to improve their look and to make cleaning easier. But these were only one-time solutions; McDonald's appreciated that cleanliness is a dynamic process. To accomplish that, the company needed to change its procedures to make dining area and bathroom cleanups a greater day-to-day priority for employees. It also needed to introduce some of the latest electronic handheld tools to regularly test cooking surfaces to make sure they were at the highest levels of cleanliness and hygiene.

Improve Value. After fifty-five years in business selling billions of items, McDonald's understood as well as anyone that "value" is a matter of perception, and less a science than an art. For some customers, value is synonymous with "inexpensive" or "sold at a discount" below the standard price. For others, a good value is a perceived "high-end" product sold at a lower price than its usual source (a sit-down restaurant, a health-food store). The reinvention of its menu offered a perfect moment for McDonald's to satisfy both customer types by offering a Dollar Menu at the bottom end of the pricing scale and health-food items at the top.

Improve Marketing. All of these changes presented McDonald's with the opportunity to recast itself both as a responsible corporation that exhibited concern for the health of its customers and the favorite fast food restaurant of one's childhood, where one could return again and again to enjoy a similar experience. These two themes would offer the added value of shifting McDonald's message from products back to a renewed focus on its customers.

SITTING PRETTY

Beginning in 2003, McDonald's began to execute all five components of its Plan to Win. New store openings dropped from 1,000 per year to fewer than 500.[10] It shed its noncore businesses, and set about renovating its existing stores and implementing a massive company-wide revised training program for all 1.5 million of its employees. The menu was rewritten as planned to incorporate value meals, healthy choices, and premium items.

The company also embarked on a two-pronged advertising campaign. One, designed to address growing negative consumer perceptions, focused on proper nutrition and quality (and was backed by a Web site dedicated to good eating habits), sponsored local sports teams, and encouraged physical activity programs for adults and kids. The second campaign, built around the theme "i'm lovin' it," combined a pitch for McDonald's improved products with the idea of being forever young and keeping McDonald's as a lifelong favorite place to eat.

Nobody captured McDonald's new attitude toward its customers— and the company's return to the demand-driven principles that first made it a success—better than CEO Jim Skinner, who told us, "I think of McDonald's again as a fifteen-cent hamburger, adjusted for inflation."[11]

The result? After hitting bottom in 2002, McDonald's revenues and income both returned to their historic upward march, even during a growing recession. Since 2004, McDonald's total sales have increased from $50.8 billion to $72.3 billion in 2009, a jump of more than 42 percent.[12] Meanwhile, net income has increased by 96 percent, from $2.3 billion to $4.5 billion, during the same period.[13]

At the same time, the number of restaurants has grown more modestly, by just 6.5 percent, during the same period,[14] underscoring McDonald's newfound commitment to "better, not bigger." In the process, because overconstruction of new restaurants is no longer drawing away business from established franchises, average sales per McDonald's restaurant jumped from $1.6 million to $2.2 million during this same period.[15] This, in turn, means improved cash flow for franchisees and more volume for suppliers.

Most important of all, McDonald's was revitalized by all of these changes and this new strategy. Customers could feel the change the moment they walked in. Employees felt it, too, and ultimately the stock market felt it as well. McDonald's was one of only two Dow Jones Industrial Average stocks that ended the recession year of 2008 with a gain[16] and also outperformed all of its fast food competitors.

And, McDonald's Plan to Win was global, so the improvements around the world came just in time to shore up revenues as the United States slid into a recession. This also proved a huge success. The *Chicago Tribune*, covering the story, quoted an industry analyst as saying: "It's just really good execution across the brand and across the globe . . . They took a lot of pages from their playbook here and implemented them overseas."[17]

Having begun the decade looking old and increasingly obsolete, McDonald's finished it revitalized and once again on top. The discipline and energy that McDonald's applied to its Plan to Win (what we call its "thesis for winning") has made it a growth company again. The return of QSCV (plus F) is already paying off handsomely.

HAMBURGER HEAVEN

It hasn't been easy, but McDonald's has transformed itself into a demand-driven corporation. To appreciate how far the company has come, let's briefly revisit the list of characteristics of such a company from the Introduction, and see how McDonald's fits.

First, and most important, the company has shifted from a focus almost purely on supply (i.e., expanding the franchise as quickly as possible) to one that makes its first priority satisfying the demands of customers in terms of service, quality, product offerings, and cleanliness. In McDonald's CEO Jim Skinner's words, "We want to get better, not just bigger. To better satisfy customer demand rather than just opening more restaurants."[18]

The company and all its stakeholders also now have a better idea of what it will take to win and of their role in achieving that victory (what we call a "thesis for winning" and "mental models" in Chapter 7). And indeed, the company works harder than ever before to maintain an alignment in goals and direction between the corporation and its franchisees, suppliers, and employees. So deep is this commitment that the company was willing to sell off some fast-growing new businesses (e.g., Chipotle) in order to return to a focus on satisfying demand for its core brand.

To assure a commitment to the customer, McDonald's has also developed its own proprietary framework—*The Customer Satisfaction Opportunity Score*—which measures each restaurant on five critical factors of customer satisfaction. There is no better way to guarantee how well you are satisfying demand than by asking your customers, and then sharing the results with everyone in the organization from the CEO to the employee at the counter who first greets the customer during what McDonald's refers to as "the moment of truth."[19]

McDonald's is also looking beyond current demand to latent and emerging demand, trying harder than ever to anticipate changing customer tastes and lifestyles. One immediate result of this strategy is a growing emphasis on the drive-through window as consumers increasingly shift to that mode of shopping. The same research into latent demand has led to other new McDonald's services, including being open twenty-four hours and offering salads, snacks, and the new line of premium coffee drinks.

By focusing on customer demand, and then using state-of-the-art networking to share new information on that demand with both franchisees and suppliers, McDonald's has developed a collaboratı system that continually aligns all of its participants with the customer, but—as we've seen by the changing menu—orients McDonald's existing supply chain as well.

And while from one perspective these changes can be seen as revolutionary for McDonald's, from another it is merely the company returning to its roots with Ray Kroc, and to what originally made the company great.

THE NEW IMPERATIVE

The single most important lesson to take away from McDonald's remarkable turnaround is this: *In a world where supply is growing ever more efficient while demand is flattening or even contracting, understanding demand becomes the new imperative for how companies will compete and win.*

In the next few pages, we will show you how the ratio of supply and demand, in equilibrium around the globe for a half-century, has now become unbalanced,[20] and why that disequilibrium of oversupply requires a fundamental rethinking of your business strategy. You can still win, even in a time of dwindling demand, if your customers and consumers want what you supply more than your competitors' products and services. But that in turn will require a deep understanding of demand that will guide you to create the products and services that best satisfy your most profitable customers and consumers.

Furthermore, with the high levels of competition that characterize the present and the foreseeable future, the margin for error has gone down and the need for precision has gone up. In particular, precision in understanding exactly which pools of customers and consumers offer the greatest potential profitability for your company has increased in importance as well as degree. With this knowledge you can align your supply and your resources to better satisfy this demand and thus capture the largest possible share of the most profitable markets.

THE DEMAND-DRIVEN ECONOMY

*Why the Relationship Between
Supply and Demand Is Changing*

Just how did McDonald's know that it was time to introduce salads and to keep their stores open twenty-four hours per day? How did Apple know that consumers wanted to bring the best of mobile phones and PCs together into a device that might ultimately reinvent both industries? How did IBM know that it was time to evolve from the world's largest and most respected technology hardware supplier to one of the world's most respected technology services providers?

The simple answer is that each of these companies understood, in a very deep way, the facts, the economics, and the content of what their customers and consumers *demanded*. Companies like these, which win on a continual basis, operate above all by understanding demand at the higher market and sector levels. By comparison, companies that struggle to compete quarter to quarter operate at lower levels of understanding that encompass only basic customer needs and product attributes. The result is that informed by an understanding that markets evolve at the level of current, latent, and emerging demand, demand-driven companies consistently have a larger and longer perspective than their competition.

The demand-driven company not only thinks about today and tomorrow, but next year and the next five years. The supply-driven company only thinks about today, tomorrow, and the end of the quarter.

Though what these great companies do may appear to be some sort of magic, it is in fact the result of a business model that operates beyond the simple—and increasingly risky—strategy of "asking customers what they want." These great companies see trends and recognize patterns forming in their markets, their category, among their different customer segments—and even outside their businesses, in adjacent markets and across the entire culture—to develop hypotheses about what those customers *will* want. Only then are they in a position to query customers—and even then, only the right customers—and begin to align current strategies, resource allocation, products, and other offers to intercept this demand as it approaches. This is a far more powerful and multifaceted approach to identifying your *real* customers than was ever before possible. And the companies that can accomplish this complex feat—who speak the language of customer demand, not merely customer need—are rewarded with the ability to continuously create organic growth. It is an approach that you can follow.

———

One last comment: We've been talking an awful lot about *demand* and *supply*. We have already given you an expanded definition of demand. Now we need a good definition of supply, as the changing interaction between the two is, after all, at the heart of this book.

Supply is the sum total of what the provider does to satisfy the customer's demand, both physical and emotional. It is important to recognize that supply is not just the product itself, but also all the elements that support the product, including price, packaging, messaging, the channels of distribution, customer service, and the brand. Price is generally seen as part of the supply proposition, even though economists typically view it as the outcome of the intersection of demand and supply. (Note that this is not inconsistent with our perspective, as demand equivalently determines volume sold at the price offered as part of supply.)

To give a concrete example of our definition, the iPhone's supply is not just the instrument itself, but also includes its almost jewel case–like packaging, the distinctive connection with the Apple brand, the thousands of downloadable applications—many of them free and designed by users, its channels of distribution, the many accessories available, and its after-purchase support, to name a few.

Now let's establish the context for the new demand-driven economy.

TURNING POINTS

The relatively stable, growing economy that the developed world has enjoyed almost uninterrupted since the end of World War II is transitioning to a new economic order. You can see the signs of change almost every day in financial, business, and political news. Certainly the global economic crash that began in late 2007 indicated that significant changes were taking place, changes that would have major implications for business and how companies win in this new economic environment.

History teaches us that great economic and social revolutions arrive slowly, almost invisibly, growing ever larger beneath the calm surface of the status quo, until they either surface quietly (if we're lucky) or burst into the open during a crisis they helped to precipitate (if we're not). Either way, one day you look around you and realize that everything has changed, the rules have been rewritten, and the business world operates in a very different way than before.

In the vast and complex world of business, that turning point has been coming on fast now since the turn of the twenty-first century, and it portends equally transformative effects on industries, the customers they sell to, and end consumers. Unfortunately, the events of 2008 to 2010 suggest that the transition to the next economic era is not going to come easy. We've already had one global economic crisis now caused in large part by unchecked attempts to create both greater supply *and* demand than the world's markets could take: an increase in the supply of houses; an increase in demand for mortgages; an increase in the supply of collateralized debt obligations (CDOs) and greater demand on banks to assume more risk; more demand for uncontrolled derivatives; and less supply of the regulation and oversight to control the resulting financial chaos.

If we don't begin to understand what is going on and respond intelligently, there will be more crises to come. That's one reason why in writing this book, despite the innovative ideas we propose, we grounded everything in the most basic rules of economics . . . supply and demand.

Our research suggests that we are in the midst of a four-phase transformation from a supply-based economy to a demand-based one:[1]

Market Equilibrium (1947–1990)[2]

The long aftermath of the Second World War, in which prosperity was quick to return to some regions of the world (notably North America) and not to others (Eastern Europe, Southeast Asia), created an extended period of continuous, manageable growth in demand. In the early 1950s, W. Edwards Deming and Joseph Juran emphasized manufacturing quality in addition to low cost, which led in turn to the development of new techniques, ultimately including supply chain management (SCM) in the 1980s.[3] SCM, which systematizes and tunes the process of getting components to manufacturers at the right volume, cost, and quantity, is one of the revolutionary business inventions of the twentieth century. So completely have we assimilated its philosophy, processes, and tools that we barely notice its operation inside a modern company. And we have come to believe that the equilibrium it creates is the natural state of the economy. It isn't.

Oversupply (1991–2007)[4]

The reality was that relative global equilibrium between supply and demand was itself merely a transition between one era and another. Other forces were at work as well, including an aging population in the developed world, rapid globalization following the end of the cold war, and the sudden bursts of productivity made possible by the rate of technological innovation and the Internet. This was, not surprisingly, seen as good news: the notion of general abundance and increased buying power played a major role in the boom of the 1990s. Consumer spending continued to increase, companies ramped up their operations, and a whole new infrastructure technology—the Internet—kicked off one of the biggest entrepreneurial booms in history.

But by 2000, it was becoming obvious that much of this boom was, in fact, a bubble. There was simply not enough demand to support the level of new business being created to pursue it; there were too many companies and products chasing too few customers. There were other bubbles in the years that followed, notably in residential real estate. Finally, in 2007, it all started to unravel, and before it was done, the collapse of the housing market had taken the world banking industry and the global economy with it.

Demand Contraction (2008–2009)[5]

The global economic crash, which had its beginnings in 2007 and shocked the world in 2009, represented an almost perfect economic storm. First, home ownership—the largest source of personal wealth in the United States and most other countries—plummeted in value. Record-high foreclosures took a situation already characterized by oversupply and threw thousands of new homes on the market, which further drove down prices. Unemployment, which rocketed up to more than 10 percent, further reduced demand, as did a resulting shift in consumer behavior toward greater savings (as we will see).

As the economy continued to slump, federal governments had no choice but to embark on hugely expensive stimulus programs, which in turn drove up government debt to historic levels. Servicing that debt will tie up those governments for years to come—and likely force many to increase taxes on the citizenry, further decreasing the available wealth for consumption.

For the first time in their histories, most of the world's manufacturers faced a world in which demand could no longer be depended on to grow inexorably far into the future. Instead, demand was actually shrinking or flattening dramatically in almost every category.

Demand-Driven Economy (2010 and beyond)[6]

A state of demand contraction and flattening cannot last forever. The business cycle eventually restores prosperity to consumers, which in turn ameliorates some of the reduced demand. At the same time, some companies have had to cut their production while others have become victims of the crash, which in turn has begun to reduce supply.

But that won't solve the underlying problem. And, in fact, it is only likely to become worse as two powerful new economies—China and India—further ramp up production to support their fragile prosperity, creating even more oversupply. Meanwhile, supply chain management continues to grow in efficiency. Ultimately, the people of China, India, and other emerging nations represent an immense source of new demand. But right now, they have an average annual income less than what many Americans spend each year on their utility bill. What they can do right now is sell: handcrafted items, small manufactured goods, and online labor. Years from now, these multitudes may lead the global economy to its next equilibrium, but for now they may represent a generation or more during which the ratio of supply to demand is continually tipped toward supply.

As we write this, demand is beginning to return to some markets and business categories. But there is no evidence that we will see again—at least not anytime soon—the kind of continuous growth in demand that we enjoyed for six decades after World War II. This suggests a slower growing, and yet more volatile, future for demand. As demand grows more slowly, its gains are offset by continual increases in productivity and greater access to low-cost labor in developing nations. Therefore, whatever gains are made in demand are likely to be more than outpaced by those increases in supply.

That's bad news, because whenever there's a growing ratio of supply to demand, there is downward pressure on prices and profits. Organic growth, which has always been difficult to achieve, becomes ever more elusive.

For the next several years, businesses will find themselves in a period of hypercompetition driven by flat demand and significant increases in lower-cost supply. The conclusion: companies that have a competitively advantaged understanding of profitable demand will be the winners. Indeed, for these companies the next several years will provide an opportunity.

A new business era is upon us, and whether we knew it not, it has already been affecting our professional and personal lives now for twenty years. It is not going away. Rather, after a period of transition—one that we may attenuate if remedies aren't taken soon—we will enter into a new era characterized by a restructuring of the supply-demand model we know today, one in which demand will both lead and direct the processes of supply, manufacturing, and marketing.

BEHIND THE DEMAND CONTRACTION

Let's take a closer look at why, after more than sixty years of near-continuous growth, demand suddenly contracted—and why the forces that this contraction unleashed all but guarantee that demand, even as it slowly returns, will continue to be dramatically outpaced by the rapid growth in supply for many years to come. We do this to underscore why there is no going back.

The stunning global contraction of demand that began in 2007 was something we hadn't seen since the Great Depression—and even the Great Depression was not at the same time paired with a state of oversupply.

Much of this demand contraction is driven by shrinking consumer spending. And what drove consumers to back off on their spending? The causal factors included:

• *High Levels of Unemployment and Underemployment*[7] These issues as well as prospects for a "jobless recovery" are causing greater uncertainty in the minds of business leaders and consumers all across the world. Until optimism and confidence outpace pessimism, demand will at best remain flat.

• *Declining Home Values*[8] When the housing bubble burst, an important driver of spending (and employment) went with it. Home equity loans, which had become a major force in demand expansion, virtually disappeared. Today, an enormous number of homes are worth less than the mortgages they carry. The glut of unsold homes in the United States and around the world is likely to remain large for many years to come. That in turn will keep home prices down for many years, keeping meaningful downward pressure on demand.

• *Small Business and Consumer Credit Constraints*[9] As the banking industry in the United States and much of the rest of the world neared collapse in early 2008, it appeared that the only way to save it was to pump liquidity into the system to pull it back from the brink of widespread default. This in turn set off a credit freeze, especially for small businesses and consumers. Small businesses led America out of its last four recessions, but unfortunately, with limited access to credit, these same small businesses will grow much more slowly, if at all. Small businesses may no longer be capable of creating the number of new jobs needed, especially as large corporations continue their relentless pursuit of efficiency and overhead reduction.

• *Legislation*[10] Legislation already passed, aimed at credit card issuers, is potentially a very high risk facing the U.S. economy. Banks are no longer able to appropriately price to risk, and will therefore be very conservative in extending credit to higher-risk consumers. Clearly, a balance needs to be found. However, in an economy that is driven around 70 percent by consumer spending,[11] radical legislation that reduces credit may be the definition of a law of unintended consequences.

• *Consumer Savings* Following a steady decline in the personal savings rate from its peak of 10.9 percent in 1982 to as low as 1.4 percent in 2005, the savings rate is once again broadly trending upward, reaching 3.1 percent in the first quarter of 2010.[12] While in the long term, higher savings rates lead to investment, innovation, and growth, in the near term each 1 percent increase in U.S. savings removes $109 billion from the U.S. economy.[13] Hardly a recipe for growth and demand.

All of these factors have combined to put a constraint on demand in both consumer and industrial markets. These are not just structural issues, but human and attitudinal issues as well, all of which will dampen demand for the foreseeable future.

A PRICING CRISIS

Let's add one more factor: *prices.* We are convinced that you cannot understand what is going on in the global economy today, much less what is being described in all of those popular business books, without first understanding its impact on prices. It is the hidden dynamo causing what seem to be inexplicable market shifts, dislocations, and crashes.

During the years from the end of World War II to 1990, market demand was roughly equal to industry supply—meaning that most of what was produced could be sold. Just as important, producers during this era could still practice what is known as cost-plus pricing—that is, charging prices that included the rising costs of production as well as a profit margin.

But even then, the forces of supply (including globalization, technology, channel growth, instant information) began to outstrip demand. And when those two lines crossed, the impact of the oversupply created was to significantly reduce pricing power. To understand just how big the impact was, consider these pricing power metrics for both the business-to-consumer (B2C) and business-to-business (B2B) markets over the last decade:[14]

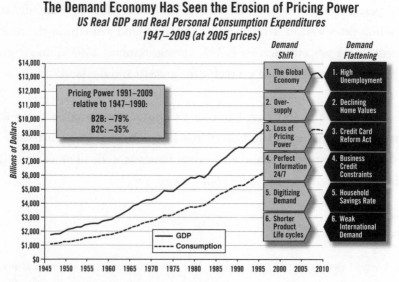

The Demand Economy Has Seen the Erosion of Pricing Power
US Real GDP and Real Personal Consumption Expenditures
1947–2009 (at 2005 prices)

Source: Bureau of Economic Analysis National Income Accounts; TCG Analysis

Ultimately, pricing is about *control*. When you lose your power to set prices to your best advantage, you also lose the ability to shape the market. You lose the ability to maximize your profits. That means you are no longer in control of your destiny. And, as every business leader knows, that is a very vulnerable—and dangerous—place to be.

THE LONG VIEW

We first saw this transformation coming more than a dozen years ago.

In 2002, Jason Green, Dr. Venkatesh Bala, and Rick Kash wrote a book, *The New Law of Demand and Supply*, that defined and described what we saw as the emerging primacy of demand over supply. In that book, we didn't abandon the historical primacy of supply and demand. On the contrary, we underscored the fact that Adam Smith, in all of his genius, got it right in *The Wealth of Nations*[15] nearly 250 years ago. In the intervening quarter-millennium, capitalism may have grown infinitely more complex but, we wrote, it remained true that the two pillars of business—supply and demand—still ruled. The most successful people, the best strategies, and the winning companies still were those that understood that fact in all of its implications.

What had changed, we argued, was the sequence: putting supply before demand, with its implied precedence, was the right thing to do in 1776 . . . and in 1976. But now, at the turn of twenty-first century, we were already seeing a major shift taking place in the global economy. By the time we wrote *The New Law of Demand and Supply*, it had become apparent just what those changes would be:

- Cycles in globalization that would be faster than anything experienced before

- Oversupply in almost every major industry sector

- A parallel loss of pricing power

- Consumers with 24/7 access to precise pricing information, ending the power of information scarcity

- Shorter product life cycles

What was emerging, we realized, was a new primacy of demand—and this shift was going in the *opposite* direction of most modern businesses, which were still trying to perfect their supply chains.

The idea of a supply chain and the notion that it could be managed scientifically, have only been around since the early 1950s (although the term "Supply Chain Management" was not coined until the 1980s).[16] But it wasn't until the 1980s,[17] when the looming threat of Japanese industry—armed with the Deming/Juran quality model and threatening to overrun the U.S. market with demonstrably superior products at lower prices—that American companies were forced to take a cold-eyed look at their underlying business model. What they saw was of great concern: significantly lower Asian labor costs, greater manufacturing efficiencies, a dedication to quality, and other macroeconomic factors had given companies in those nations a nearly insurmountable advantage. The companies of the United States and developed nations in Europe quickly concluded that their only hope was to try to match those advantages where they could—and then compete with ever greater efficiency in their supply chains.

The result was the rise of supply-chain management as a professional discipline—and a business transformation so complete that today's generation of business leaders assume it is as old as business itself, not a creation from their own youth.

Suddenly, we realized it was no longer enough to focus solely on growing one's share of the market; now success would go to those firms that intensely focused on understanding how to compete and win in an environment where the changing nature of demand was now calling the tune.

In the years since we wrote that book, every one of these predictions has come true to one degree or another—which is why these days we no longer hesitate to say that something fundamental and profound has taken place in the global economy. It is a shift so sweeping and so important that we believe that if Adam Smith were writing *The Wealth of Nations* today, he would invert his famous phrase to reflect this new reality: the Law of Demand and Supply.

Smith would surely have recognized that in a world of efficiency and oversupply (so unlike his own in the Scottish Enlightenment), it is now critical first and foremost to have a deep understanding of current, latent, and emerging demand. And he would have instantly understood that armed with this powerful insight, it would be possible to align differentiated supply in order to capture a disproportionately high share of the highest-profit demand.

Back in 2002, we kept asking ourselves: *Is this a blip on the radar screen or is it the beginning of a long-term trend?*

Eight years later, the answer is clear: we have entered into a long-term demand dominance. And while the implications of this global economic inflection are already enormous, they are likely to be even greater in the future.

So how can you only be learning now about a major economic shift taking place around you? Quite simple. Recall that during the Industrial Revolution, some industries had fifty years or more to adapt. The same was true for the so-called Second Industrial Revolution of large factories and mass production.

Moreover, the pace of change itself is accelerating. Note that each of the intervals we just mentioned is about half the length of its predecessor. The demand economy is coming fast because *everything* is coming faster. In the age of Google and Bing and terabytes of market data, we (and just as important, our competitors) don't need decades to determine that a change is taking place. These days, the time between an important news event and its impact around the world can be measured not in decades, or even months, but in *seconds*—again underscoring the fact that information is yet one more thing that has evolved from scarcity to oversupply.

It's a bit of an overworked cliché to compare any new economic transformation to the Industrial Revolution and other points of inflection in the past. Nevertheless, it isn't an idle effort to see if we can find parallels between the changes that drove the Industrial Revolution and the changes driving the demand economy today.

History shows that most of the major transformations in industry, including the first and second Industrial Revolutions, were sparked by five events:

- *A transformation in labor* from craft guilds to assembly lines; the rise of the management and professional classes

- *A jump in productivity* due to both the transformation in labor and the invention of new technologies and tools (the factory, vertical integration, computers, and networks)

- *A sudden expansion in markets*

- *A change in where and how work was done*, especially the movement of workers from farms and villages to city centers

- *A burst of entrepreneurship*

Sound familiar? In the "age of demand," the same five factors are at work—and can be readily identified. For example:

1. A Transformation in Labor The last twenty years have seen a continuous outflow of labor from traditional developed nations such as the United States and the United Kingdom to traditional developing nations such as India and China, with the latter countries in turn enjoying historically high rates of growth.[18]

2. A Jump in Productivity In the last three quarters of 2009, U.S. labor productivity grew on average more than 7 percent—more than three times higher than the historical average since 1948.[19] Are people working harder? Sure, but not enough to account for this astounding jump, one of the biggest since such measurements began. At some point early in the new century, the combination of personal computers, networks, the Web, and immense libraries of software finally meshed with a new generation of tech-savvy workers and everything took off. This kind of torrid pace can't go on forever—but before it slows again, every notion about how human beings work will have to be rewritten.

3. A Sudden Expansion in Markets It took the global marketplace more than 20,000 years to reach one billion consumer participants. It took only twenty years to reach the second billion. And it will only take a couple more years, until about 2012, to bring on board the third billion.[20] Many of those third billion are beginning to sell their goods on eBay and buy items from Amazon using low-cost cell phones with Internet access. Ultimately, in a generation or two, these multitudes will have enough economic power to evolve the world beyond the demand economy to something we can't yet imagine. For the moment, however, they are helping create our current crisis of oversupply.

4. A Change in Where and How Work Is Done Today, work can take place almost anywhere, with multimedia access to databases, tools, marketing and sales materials, and interoffice communication. The physical boundaries of most companies have been torn down. This has inevitably changed the way companies do business. The hierarchal corporation, the mainstay of the industrial world, is disappearing rapidly, and is unlikely to ever return.

5. A Burst of Entrepreneurship Economic downturns have historically been boom times for new company creation. In the new global, networked economy, entrepreneurship has also become a lot easier, once again thanks to access—which enables start-ups to recruit talent and search for investors around the world. The result, as Ken Auletta wrote in his book *Googled: The End of the World As We Know It*,[21] is a new reality in which the biggest fear of even the largest and most up-to-date companies is that what two college students are doing in some garage might render their entire industry obsolete.

Frankly, any one of these five factors would be enough to provoke a major transformation in an economy. That all are present argues for a major revolution. The demand economy and its deep implications for how to manage and win is decidedly *not* a blip on the radar screen.

THE FORGOTTEN CUSTOMER

So where was demand during all of these years of focus on supply? Mostly taken for granted—seemingly arising out of nowhere to respond to the goods and services you were able to supply.

It was only in the early 1990s that American industry had a revelation regarding the customer. In retrospect, we can see it now as the first stage in the demand revolution. Behind this breakthrough was a spate of business books, all saying essentially the same thing: "Go ask your customer." At the time, the notion was shocking—not least because it was assumed that companies were already talking to their customers.

In the end, the celebration of the customer was a brief one, because it quickly became obvious that if you had to ask your customer what he or she wanted, it was already too late. If they were telling you, they were telling your competitors as well.

But many companies still rely for their understanding of demand almost solely on what their customers tell them. This strategy is dangerous because it makes companies increasingly time vulnerable. Response times get shorter by the year, and more than one company has found itself in trouble after deciding to pursue a new product opportunity suggested by customers—and then watching as competitors in the Far East and elsewhere get that same product to market in a matter of weeks. At best, a policy that is largely reliant on "asking the customer" can enable you to keep up with the competition, but never get ahead of it.

Our belief is that the key to success today is to develop a hypothesis about the future of demand *while it is still forming*. That is, while their competitors are asking questions about present demand, companies that win are trying to determine where demand will be tomorrow, next year, and five years from now. They devote their energies and resources to looking not just at current, but latent and emerging, demand. And they do so on many levels:

1. They use macroeconomics to look across multiple markets, to draw lessons to apply in their own markets.

2. They look at customer and consumer trends (lifestyle, work style, fads, demographics), to anticipate how to interact with emerging trends.

3. They look at adjacent categories, to see what they can learn from best practices, successes, and failures from businesses similar to their own.

4. They look at the most profitable segments of their own customers, to detect even small variations in their behavior and buying patterns.

5. They take advantage of the real-time ability to monitor buzz on the Internet, to get an over-the-horizon view of emerging opportunities. They leverage new techniques such as crowdsourcing not only to help them gather timely knowledge about demand, but also to enlist their most desirable customers in the design of the product itself.

The sum total of all of these investigations enables these demand-oriented companies to formulate new hypotheses about where this demand is going, and to make these hypotheses more insightful and more future oriented than anything they could derive from merely "asking the customers."

Only now, armed with these disciplined, differentiated, and insightful hypotheses, do these companies at last query their customers for their comments. But here again, it is not so simple. It isn't just any customers they ask, but only the ones they want: the most profitable customers.

QUESTIONS OF DEMAND

It doesn't matter if you are a newspaper stand, a printing company, a semiconductor giant, or a global packaged goods manufacturer. In the demand economy, the fate of your enterprise now boils down to a simple question:

What do you know about the demand of your most profitable customers that your competitors don't know?

It is the precise and strategic answer to this question that enables you to make and align differentiated supply so that it better satisfies the demand of your most profitable customers. Further, that it satisfies that demand better than the endless amounts of untargeted and undifferentiated lower-cost supply coming from anywhere and everywhere.

In the demand economy, low-cost supply is necessary but not sufficient in order to win. Real success comes from the combination of understanding demand and then creating the right product, the right package, the right price, and the right communications and total messaging, so that your total proposition aligns with that demand. This is the very definition of pricing power—and it is available to everybody. It is identifying the high-profit demand and then differentiating your product that enables you to earn high levels of profit.

———

Let's go back to that simple, but critical, question: *What do you know about the demand of your most profitable customers that your competitors don't know?* Do you know the answer? If not, can you find that answer? If you can't, you can at least take heart in the fact that your predicament is shared by most companies—even some of world's largest corporations.

This shouldn't be surprising. In a world focused for generations on supply, that wasn't a question most companies ever needed to ask of themselves. But today it is.

Perhaps the best way to begin answering this question is to break it down into four more focused questions:

1. Who are my most profitable customers?

2. What is their unsatisfied current, latent, and emerging demand?

3. How do I differentiate my products and services so I better satisfy the demand of those most profitable customers?

4. What is the action plan so I can align the people inside of my company to satisfy the demand for all of our customers outside of my company?

In the new demand economy, these four questions—and the larger question they solve—may be the most important that your company asks. They are now at *the heart of your business strategy*. How you answer will define your business model, help you architect your business strategy, and enable your company to continually grow revenues and profits.

With entire pools of demand evaporating in the current economy, and others becoming commoditized and low-profit in the face of global oversupply, finding those highest-profit customer clusters, growing them, and then hanging on to them for dear life may decide your company's future.

You have little choice but to do this, because the entire business environment has changed. Our current situation will improve only slowly, over years, perhaps taking even a generation or more. It will take years to restore all of that lost wealth, all of those lost jobs, and all of those new companies that would have led us through the next economic boom but which either failed or were never founded. In the meantime, we face a long-term disequilibrium,[22] with the gap continuing to grow between a still-increasing supply and a flattened (at best) demand.

This is a game-changing turnabout for the business world. Until now, much of the modern world economy has been built on a simple equation for success:

Grow at equal to or just above GDP growth, while at the same time cutting your supply chain costs by 4 to 5 percent annually, and you will enjoy double-digit growth forever.

But in this new business environment, this old tried-and-true approach is no longer sufficient, as evidenced by the fact that the dominant companies in each new economic era are often replaced by new companies that emerge during these inflection points. The list of once-great companies—indeed, household names—that dominated their markets but then failed to adapt to a new economic order and let smaller rivals eclipse them is stunning: Lehman Brothers, Keds, Woolworth, Control Data, Sears, Zenith, Polaroid, Digital Equipment, AOL . . . the list goes on and on.

In other words, intervals like the one in which we currently find ourselves are not merely "hard times"; they are also periods of great opportunity, determining the emerging rules of success and failure and welcoming some enterprises through while holding others back. They rewrite the handbook on how companies win.

THE THINGS YOU KEEP

The first question we need to ask is: *What survives?*

No new economic era has ever represented a complete break from what came before. We read about the Industrial Revolution, with its mass migration of farm laborers to the cities to work in factories—but if you had lived during that era you would have barely noticed the slow and subtle change.

The same will be true of the transition to the new era before us. This change too will be almost invisible: companies will go about their business pretty much the way they always have; the only difference will be that some find themselves with profits below the industry average and market shares that are slowly being chipped away. Other companies—including some that don't now exist—will enjoy greater-than-industry-average profits and will relentlessly capture more and more of the market . . . until one day it becomes undeniable that a profound change has occurred, there is a new order of industry-leading firms, and once-important companies will be almost forgotten.

Here then are the critical factors to long-term business success that were true in the past and that we believe will remain in place.

1. Understanding Your Customers No company that has failed to know its customers has ever survived for long. That isn't going to change. Rather, the need to understand your customers is about to become the minimum ante to stay in the game. It is certainly no longer a recipe for winning. As we transition to the demand economy, understanding demand becomes a critical first step in truly understanding the motivations, dreams, desires, and needs of your customers. Why? Because demand forms long before potential customers can even articulate their needs. Anticipating demand is one of the greatest sources of competitive advantage any business can have. We typically find that when you simply ask customers what they want, you are already too late, because they have answered the exact same question for your competitors. The new challenge is to figure out what those same customers *will* want.

2. Superior Leadership and Management It is a fact of life that the best people create and run the best companies. What will change is the skill set those "best" entrepreneurs and executives will need to succeed. The successful business leaders of the new demand economy will have added a whole set of new skills that give them a greater under-standing of the management of demand.

3. Supply Chain Management   Surprised? We just declared the pri-macy of demand and the transition to the demand economy—but we never said that supply chain management was no longer needed for success; only that it was no longer the decisive factor it once was. The sheer power of supply chain management to bring products to market profitably is undiminished—only now that supply must be tempered, channeled, and directed by an equivalent attention to the demand side of the equation. Your supply chain can't truly be optimized unless you thoroughly understand the demand it is built to serve. What is needed going forward is a new partnership between the emerging demand chain and the traditional supply chain.

4. Alignment and Execution   No organization can win if its parts are not all aligned to execute the same strategy and achieve the same goals. Even the "perfect" strategy within a competitively advantaged busi-ness model will ultimately fail if the organization is not fully aligned internally and does not understand how to execute the strategy, or if it works at cross-purposes. The company that has not aligned its internal resources in pursuit of a precisely defined goal is wasting resources it can no longer afford to squander. And the company that can't execute with ever greater speed is one that risks being left behind.

5. Leveraging Technological Change   For the last half century, the world has lived, often without knowing it, under the regime of two "laws" of technology. Moore's law[23] isn't really a law at all, but a com-mitment by the semiconductor industry to continue doubling the power/performance, miniaturization, and price reduction of computer chips every two to three years—and there is every reason to believe it will continue to do so until at least the middle of this century. Met-calfe's law[24] says that the value of any network increases exponentially with the addition of each new user. [You'll see the power of Metcalfe's law in Chapter 8 where we introduce the new network of the demand chain.] If Moore's law underlies the breathless pace of change in modern life, Metcalfe's law propels us toward ever greater interconnectedness—the Internet and the social networking companies such as Twitter and Facebook of the so-called Web 2.0 world.

THE THINGS YOU'LL NEED

That's what you keep as we enter the demand economy, but what do you need to add to your business model and to your daily operations to remain competitive?

First up is a series of operating principles and behaviors that are natural and easy to understand and accomplish. These aren't radically new concepts, but rather principles for how to think, act, and manage to compete and win in the very fast-moving demand economy.

How do you accomplish this change from a supply-based organization to one that is demand based? It starts not by what you ask people to *do*, but rather how you ask them to *think*. The wonder of the human brain is that it responds first and then directs the parts of our body to do what is best, given the context and the circumstances.

Simply said: *If you want to change the way a company acts, you must first change the way its people think.*

And what should they start thinking about?

1. The Primacy of Demand Just as supply chain management was fifty years ago, *demand is the new game changer.* You can't win anymore through great supply chain management alone; it remains necessary, but it is no longer sufficient. Today, almost every industry and category is in a significant oversupply situation, and any company that expects to maintain strong profitability and outpace its competitors must compete on demand. Demand now rules, and it will for years to come.

2. Adding the Fifth P: *Precision* For forty years, most business students have been taught the four *P*'s of marketing: product, price, place, and promotion. This model has proven to be remarkably influential and enduring. But to win in this new competitive environment we need to add one more *P* to the mix: precision. The greater the precision in analyzing demand, the tighter the alignment between what you want to sell and what the customer wants to buy.

3. Innovation as a Science of Demand   In the demand economy, a spirit of innovation must now permeate the entire organization. It is "total innovation." It is the best way for a company to identify new opportunities, marshal the talent and resources it will need to attack those opportunities, and restructure itself to quickly and effectively respond to newly discovered sources of demand.

Indeed, the best definition we know for successful innovation is to *find unsatisfied profitable demand and fulfill it.* And it won't be just R&D developing new products either; now every department, from sales to service to manufacturing and marketing, will have to be part of the team, key players in the search for total innovation.

4. Developing a Clear Thesis for Winning   One of the key characteristics of successful companies is that most have a powerful thesis for how they will win in the marketplace that can be expressed in simple terms the entire organization can understand. While the thesis is typically built from in-depth analyses of demand, customers, competitors, the marketplace, core competencies, and other critical factors, it is ultimately simplified for the entire organization and its external partners to understand. McDonald's has already given us an example.

5. Building the Mental Model   It is not enough to simply express your company's strategy for competing and winning against the competition. Rather, that strategy must be supported, endorsed, and believed in by the people inside the company. This is best accomplished with the creation of a clear statement of how the company will win, and then that statement must be promulgated through every part of the company until it becomes second nature to every employee. A successful Mental Model of how you will compete and win is shared through-out your organization.

6. The Rise of the Demand Chain As we will show you, it is possible to construct an apparatus on the demand side of your business that is similar in organization, sophistication, and power to the traditional supply chain.

Further, we believe that such a demand chain is capable of assuming a natural place alongside the traditional supply chain to create what can be considered a new kind of integrated business model, one in which the demand chain will make the supply chain more targeted and efficient. Ultimately, this combination will have the kind of revolution-ary impact last seen with supply chain management a half-century ago.

Those are the skills that you must keep and those that you must add (if you haven't already done so). That's why we devote a chapter to each of them; we show you tools that help you implement them and present case studies to show how winning companies have already put them to use.

WINNING IN A NEW WORLD

This then is the demand economy, the "flat" world that Thomas Friedman predicted.[25] We made a similar prediction of a "horizontal" economy in a speech before the Association of National Advertisers back in 2002.[26] What we said then is even more true now: the critical factor defining the demand economy is that virtually every company in the world has access—to talent, money, expertise, customers and consumers, labor, and information—in ways that could not have been imagined just a few years ago. Access is now the greatest enabler and equalizer in modern business.

The current outpouring of supply doesn't equal success—a fact still lost on most executives. So how do you win in the face of this onslaught of ever more, ever cheaper supply? By having a proprietary understanding of profitable demand—current, latent, and emerging—so that your supply will better satisfy demand. Sound difficult? Let us show you, through an almost biblical example, how easy it is to win when you have unique insights into demand.

Ten years ago water, dirt, and air were free, omnipresent, and almost perfect. Today, thanks to an understanding of demand, water, dirt, and air are three of the fastest growing and most profitable product categories in the business world. Yet nowhere is there more supply than in water, dirt, and air. If water, dirt, and air—the only things present when Adam and Eve showed up—can become highly profitable in the face of overwhelming supply, then surely your business can as well.

So while it is still best to be number one or two in your category, getting there—and even more, *staying* there—will become more and more challenging in an economy where supply is growing ever faster, demand is flat or contracting, and new and unexpected competitors are attacking from every direction.

The old rules will still apply—be the low-cost producer, hire the best people, continually innovate, understand your customers' needs—but they are no longer enough. You must find a way to defeat the threat of that flat to downward demand curve, and do so in a way that enables you to build defenses against those multiplying competitive threats, both visible and yet to emerge.

PART II

STRATEGY

THREE

DEMAND PROFIT POOLS

A Demand-Based Framework for Growing Your Business

A number of years ago, we were contacted by a very successful company in the dog food industry to see if we could identify an untapped market to spark new growth opportunities.

The standard view in the industry at that time was that the dog food market was essentially characterized by just two criteria:

- The size and/or breed of dog, or what might be called "dog-o-graphics"

- The form of food (dry/bagged or wet/canned), or "form preferences"

Given these criteria, it's really not surprising that our client—along with the rest of the dog food industry—segmented dog owners into the most rudimentary groups: owners of large dogs, who needed large bags or cans of food; owners of medium-sized dogs, who needed medium-sized bags or cans; and owners of small dogs, who needed small bags or cans. That's it. It was a market-segmentation schema that offered few insights, and absolutely no *proprietary* insights. Essentially, in each of those six segments, every company competed on the same basis using the same view of the market. It was decidedly not an environment for high profit growth or breakthrough innovation.

This is a good place to demonstrate the difference between market segments and demand profit pools. In segments, as this traditional view of the dog food category demonstrates, customers are differentiated on the basis of demographics or behavior, which is quite logical but unfortunately not very actionable. On the other hand, demand profit pools organize customers into groups based on the demand they want to satisfy, on the "why" behind the decisions they make, and on the profitability they represent.

While segments are convenient and logical, they don't reveal the deeper reasons or beliefs behind buying decisions; they only label who is doing the purchasing and what they are buying. By contrast, demand profit pools focus primarily on the "why" underlying the purchase decision—an understanding that encompasses both demographics and an understanding of past purchasing behavior. Perhaps most important, demand profit pools also create an understanding of the different economic opportunities (i.e., how potential profits vary) within each customer group.

Aggregating all of the individual demand profit pools for an industry or market provides a complete picture of the customer opportunities within that market. We call this consolidated view of demand profit pools the "demand landscape." Why do we call it a landscape? Because a landscape painting captures everything ahead of you in one sweeping view that encompasses the hills, rivers, towns, lakes, and whatever else is on the horizon. Like a painting, a demand landscape depicts current, latent, and emerging consumer demand, profitability, competitors, brands, channels, innovation opportunities, packaging, media habits, price sensitivity, and other critical metrics.

Being dog lovers ourselves, we were anxious to understand how dog food buyers actually thought about their purchasing decisions and thus how the market for dog food was really organized. It quickly became apparent that consumer decisions in this business were, in fact, *not* primarily driven by the size and breed of dog owned but rather by the type of relationship owners sought with their dog. In retrospect, it made perfect sense.

Here's the demand landscape we developed[1] with the five distinct demand profit pools we identified arranged by the type of relationship sought by each owner:

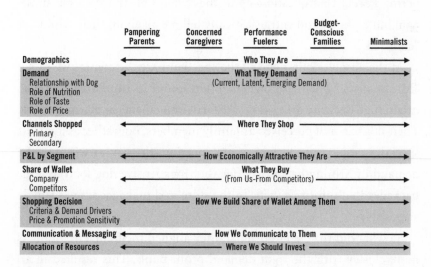

Dog Food Demand Landscape
Relationship to Dog

Dog as Love Object ← → *Dog as Functional*

	Pampering "Parents"	Concerned Caregivers	Performance Fuelers	Budget-Conscious Families	Minimalists
Relationship to Dog	➤ Dog as child	➤ Dog as part of family	➤ Dog as active partner	➤ Dog as pet	➤ Dog as farm implement
Price Sensitivity	➤ Low	➤ Moderate	➤ Low	➤ Moderate	➤ High
P&L by Segment	➤ High	➤ Moderate	➤ High	➤ Low	➤ Lowest
Geodemographic Skews	➤ Empty nesters	➤ Upscale families	➤ Singles, young families	➤ Mid-market families	➤ Larger rural households
Dog-o-Graphic Skews	➤ Small purebreds	➤ Loveable mutts ➤ Some purebreds	➤ Large purebreds	➤ Respected mutts	➤ Utilitarian hounds
Benefits Sought	➤ Buy what the dog likes best, human food characteristics	➤ Fun, variety, quality balanced with nutrition	➤ Nutrition, performance	➤ Basic nutrition, convenience	➤ Buy least expensive brands, large sizes
Sources of Information	➤ Self, family	➤ Retailer	➤ Vet ➤ Retailer	➤ Retailer	

	Pampering Parents	Concerned Caregivers	Performance Fuelers	Budget-Conscious Families	Minimalists
Demographics	←	Who They Are			→
Demand Relationship with Dog Role of Nutrition Role of Taste Role of Price	←	What They Demand (Current, Latent, Emerging Demand)			→
Channels Shopped Primary Secondary	←	Where They Shop			→
P&L by Segment	←	How Economically Attractive They Are			→
Share of Wallet Company Competitors	←	What They Buy (From Us-From Competitors)			→
Shopping Decision Criteria & Demand Drivers Price & Promotion Sensitivity	←	How We Build Share of Wallet Among Them			→
Communication & Messaging	←	How We Communicate to Them			→
Allocation of Resources	←	Where We Should Invest			→

Suddenly, our client had an entirely new and actionable understanding of what dog food people bought, why they bought it, and—perhaps most important—the profitability of each of the demand profit pools. This view of the dog-food buyer landscape was unique, something no other competitor had ever done before. It produced unique insights for our client that, in turn, resulted in their making strategic decisions, putting them on a path no other competitor had traveled before. They had gained a distinct competitive advantage.

The demand profit pool that most captured our attention was the "Pampering Parents." As is often the case with these discoveries, once we saw the results it was obvious that the truth had been before our eyes all along. Who are the Pampering Parents? These are the folks (and the description includes some of us and no doubt many of you) who look upon their dogs as children. They anthropomorphize their dogs, talk to them, and overall treat them like a favored child.

Once we really got to know this group, we found we could spot them and their pets in almost any crowd. We even made a tidy sum betting friends that a given stranger at a restaurant, ball game, or bar would have a photograph of their dog with them. I merely had to ask a Pampering Parent that question—and they would break into a big smile, haul out a photo, and enthusiastically tell me all about their "child" or "children."

At the absolute other end of the spectrum are the owners we called "Minimalists." For these owners, often found in rural areas but also urban high-security areas, dogs are farm implements or alarm systems. Their dogs are not perceived as family members, but rather as low-cost specialty employees. As you might imagine, the key to winning the demand of Minimalists is to offer very inexpensive dog food in large packages that minimize trips to the store and make feeding as simple as possible.

So what did the client do? First, they aligned their current products more closely with the right demand profit pools. This resulted in an optimized portfolio strategy that aligned each brand with the most attractive demand profit pool. By sharpening the focus of each brand, the client created greater distinctions between brands so that they were not competing with themselves. These actions took place immediately, largely by improving messaging and offers at the point of sale on the retail store shelf. Importantly, these quick wins generated both the funding and the confidence to make more involved improvements in other aspects of the offer.

In some cases, we found that better satisfying the needs of attractive demand profit pools required changes to messaging, packaging, price points, or even the product itself. For example, as you might imagine, Pampering Parents were highly price insensitive. Improvements to product quality, packaging, and positioning aimed at Pampering Parents allowed for even higher price premiums and greater profits. After careful testing and refinement, these improvements and "renovations" to existing products were rolled out to all of the client's retail channels in the near term.

But the most exciting opportunity was with the "Performance Fuelers." These are the folks who live an active, healthy lifestyle (runners, bikers, backpackers) and include their dogs in these activities. What makes these consumers particularly interesting is like the Pampering Parents they are willing to pay a premium price in order for their dogs to eat "only the best." Unlike the Pampering Parents, however, the "best" from the Performance Fuelers' perspective meant a balance of healthy nutrition and a taste their dog would love. The Performance Fuelers scrutinize the dog food they buy; they study the ingredients list and nutrition table, and they study their dogs' eating habits to make sure the food is good tasting as well. Importantly, they want new options to deliver on that balance—and that is the best prerequisite for both product differentiation and high profit margins.

In order to meet the demand of Performance Fuelers we realized a new-to-the-world product was required. At the time, Performance Fuelers were not at all satisfied with the few choices they had for providing the health and nutrition they sought for their dogs. Most options were so focused on healthfulness at the expense of taste that their dogs wouldn't eat them. Feeding time became a real chore that pitted owners who wanted to do the right thing against dogs who wouldn't eat. To make matters worse, these healthful options charged a steep premium.

Prior to the demand landscape we developed, our clients had not realized that the Performance Fuelers' demand profit pool existed, so of course, they had no idea how large the pool was, how dissatisfied those consumers were, or how profitable they could be to serve. Now that we knew what was most important to Performance Fuelers and how they made decisions, we understood exactly how to develop the optimal product for their demand, a product that would balance healthy nutrition with taste at a price owners considered well worth every penny.

The result? The introduction of a whole new dog food brand, the most successful new product ever introduced by this manufacturer. It is not so much a product as a platform for innovation that has resulted in an entire portfolio of new products including foods to help dogs lose weight, foods designed for a radiant coat, and even healthy dog snacks. Next time you're at a pet store, look at the product differentiation sparked in recent years by this company's decision to pursue a high-nutrition, premium dog food. As for the client itself, it remains one of the most profitable—and innovative—brands in the marketplace.

Perhaps over time the client would have found the demand for healthier, more nutritious dog foods to fuel performance. But it is unlikely that they would have preempted the competition and grown the brand so dramatically if they were simply looking at dog-o-graphics or products purchased.

DIFFERENTIATED DEMAND

Imagine how your business would benefit if you had a single integrated framework to:

- Find the high-profit consumers who can raise your margins and revenues

- Understand current, latent, and emerging demand

- Determine which channels are growing and which channels are slowing

- Assess where your competitors are strong and where they are weakest

- Understand the media habits of your most important consumers

- Identify the best potential opportunities for innovation

- Build a financial model for resource allocation to drive faster growth

- Develop insights about the demand of your most profitable customers that your competitors don't know

When you build an effective demand landscape and understand the demand profit pools within it, all of these questions can be readily answered. Once you have this understanding, you are in a better position to satisfy the demands of the most attractive of these demand profit pools. You can use your knowledge and understanding to align your differentiated brands and products so that you capture a larger percentage of the profitable demand than your competitors. The framework also becomes the basis for how to manage your brands and products as a portfolio. And because it includes information about virtually every function within the company, from finance to manufacturing to marketing and sales, it is the integrated framework through which all can understand, talk about, and manage the activities of their operations.

Demand profit pools exist because demand is not homogeneous. Indeed, in the world of demand, no size fits all, which ultimately means that in any given market there are likely to be multiple distinct pools of demand. Mercedes sedans, GMC pickup trucks, Honda hybrids, and Cadillac Escalades can all be successful and profitable car brands while serving very different demand profit pools within the larger vehicle market. In our experience, most markets feature at least six different demand profit pools. That's a lot of opportunity.

Customers within those demand profit pools are attracted to both the rational and emotional benefits of these submarkets. So why the range of products? Because people have different lives, tastes, lifestyles, needs, and personal histories. They also live in different environments and are at different points in their lives. The result is a wide spectrum in both rational benefits (quality, performance, safety, comfort, eco-friendliness, mileage, power, price) and emotional rewards (status, "greenness," hipness, safety).

Demand profit pools are groups of customers who make similar decisions based on the common needs they want satisfied. Any given market, whether in consumer or business-to-business industries, will have several distinct demand profit pools. These should be defined not simply by who these customers are or what they purchase but, most important, on why they make the decisions they make. And beyond understanding the who, what, and why of customers by group, businesses that win must fully understand the economics of each demand profit pool. Determining which ones spend the most, which are most and least price sensitive, and which offer the highest and lowest profit potential are all critical to determining which demand profit pools to focus on and how to serve them.

Too many companies still try to be all things to all people and end up being very few things to very few people instead. You cannot just decide to sell everything to everyone walking through the door. That was a strategy for mediocrity in the supply era, and it is a recipe for failure now as demand flattens or declines. Today, you need the discipline to first ask *Do I want to serve the low-profit customer or the high-profit customer?* and then follow through with all the response entails. To do so is to make demand profit pools central to your proprietary view of the market and how you will compete and win within it.

When a demand landscape is done effectively, it shows exactly how to allocate resources to each demand profit pool. In short, it is a foundational framework through which you understand how to compete today and how to compete more effectively tomorrow. Unlike most strategic plans that are static documents done once per year, a demand landscape is an organic, evolving document that can be updated each quarter with new metrics to determine exactly how you are doing with each demand profit pool.

There are several demand profit pools in every single market, even in seemingly commoditized categories. No matter what industry you are in, from apparel to hospitals and from financial services to fast food restaurants, it is important to understand the demand profit pools within it. Every company should be guided by the full view of the demand landscape, accompanied by an understanding of its individual demand profit pools.

Because of this, it is possible for apparently similar companies to pursue very different business strategies, and still all be profitable. The challenge then is having the discipline to determine which demand profit pool(s) to focus on and then to align everything you do to serve that demand better than the competition. Winning means successfully:

- Identifying the most valuable of these demand profit pools

- Aligning your brands, products, messages, and resources so that you capture an increasing share of the highest-profit demand profit pools

- Innovating the right products or services for customers in these pools

- Coming up with the right pricing strategy to match the expectations of these customers

- Developing the right branding, marketing, packaging, and retail channels to match the perceptions and lifestyles of the members of these pools

In other words, your biggest opportunity is to have a proprietary understanding of current, latent, and emerging demand profit pools and then to align your business model to compete more effectively in them. To do that, you first must identify those pools—and then orient your entire business to capture the profits they offer.

This shouldn't be too surprising. After all, the pursuit of profit is the heart of business. And yet, you would be surprised how many businesses—even those that otherwise understand every tiny nuance of their industry—don't really know who their most profitable customers are and what those customers want. By comparison, the truly successful companies are those that are very clear on whom they are in business to serve, and that is the customers who offer the greatest profits. In every market we've ever worked in, the greatest success is always found where decision making and profitability track each other. And, as you'll soon see, once these criteria for high-profit demand are fully understood and adopted by a company, decision making (such as on future products) becomes much easier.

A NEW WAY TO THINK ABOUT DEMAND

This is not a small change in direction, nor merely a new tool to add to your company's collection of market analysis instruments. Rather, demand profit pools represent a strategic change in how to think about how your company can win.

As we noted at the beginning of this book, such a strategic change has happened before. What we used to think of as manufacturing has become, for strategic reasons, the supply chain. And the single most important aspect of changing this nomenclature was to reinforce the notion that what was really changing was the way the company thinks and how it works. Manufacturing was a series of siloed production steps, but the supply chain was a broader integrated set of functions, including procurement, distribution, and the information flows tying them together, that went beyond just assemble and ship. This shift in language helped to break down institutional silos and to change how people engaged in the process. The new name underscored that this was a new business paradigm.

By the same token, converting you and your company's orientation from segments to demand profit pools will also change how your company thinks and works.

In the process, this new nomenclature not only helps you focus your people on what you want to focus them on—that is, on being better at satisfying demand and driving profits—but it also becomes the basis for aligning the company internally around those new goals. That's because everybody now knows which are the most important of these demand profit pools and the priority they take in company operations.

Some well-known companies have already begun to reorient themselves toward demand profit pools. For example, Dave West, in one of his first updates for analysts as the new CEO of Hershey's, announced that a proprietary understanding of demand profit pools would be a significant driver of Hershey's success going forward. In particular, he said, the critical demand profit pool called "Engaged Exploring Munchers" would be the new focus of Hershey's efforts, and that success with these Engaged Exploring Munchers would be a key measure by which he wanted the company's success to be evaluated.[2]

To quote Dave West from that analyst update, "We have identified six core consumer groups, each with a different approach to the category. Engaged Exploring Munchers have a serious sweet tooth. Their consumption index and usage is two times their share of the population . . . they are the least price-sensitive consumers. Importantly, we know who this most profitable group is and we are actively engaged in research and insights to reposition brands to appeal specifically to them."[3]

West gets it. He knows that this demand profit pool represents a group of consumers that Hershey's has always served, but whose demand the company only recently began to understand. These Engaged Exploring Munchers turn out to represent a bit more than 10 percent of all consumers, but a significantly higher percentage of Hershey's profit.[4] Because Hershey's now knows more about this demand profit pool than anyone else, and because the company is now focused on satisfying the demand of these high-profit consumers, Dave West is confident that Hershey's can meet the needs of these consumers. The company has focused resources against the most attractive demand profit pools in order to win with these important consumers, including those Engaged Exploring Munchers. As a result, Hershey's has enjoyed several quarters of an ever increasing share of market and profit growth.[5] We'll discuss Hershey's remarkable transformation to a demand-driven company in greater detail in subsequent chapters.

*INFIRMO*GRAPHICS

The notion of demand profit pools is actually something we all experience every day. Just consider the people around you—family, friends, co-workers, customers, neighbors—and the very different decisions they make in their lives. They prefer different types of cars, foods, clothing, television shows, politicians, and music. Some are early adopters of new technologies, others are nearly Luddites. Moreover, these decisions aren't always consistent: a person who normally searches for a bargain on most things may turn around and pay a premium price for one particular product or service. That's because his demand is for the highest quality in a category of products that is important to him. For example, the audiophile who invests in a top-of-the-line sound system and an extensive collection of music may seek rock-bottom bargains across almost everything else he buys.

The goal of demand profit pool analysis is to develop an empirical understanding of the distinct decision criteria that different groups of people use to select a product or service—and then to quantify the pools of common demand to determine their size, growth potential, and profitability.

Hundreds of millions of dollars are spent by companies each year in search of the right market segments in which to compete. Unfortunately, most of those companies get very little return on their investment because that segmentation is the product of the wrong questions. The reason is that too much of this segmentation is done on the basis of demographics or past behavior, and neither criteria is very effective at determining *future* customer or consumer behavior.

For example, the practice of demographic segmentation establishes groups of consumers based on similarity in age, income, life stage (single, married, kids, empty nesters), ethnic background, gender, and education. This approach assumes that people with similar demographic profiles will have similar decision criteria and purchasing patterns. And indeed, at the most simplistic level, this holds true. This is frequently called "life stage segmentation." Indeed, some similarities can be found among consumers with comparable demographics, but they fall far short of the accuracy and actionability of grouping people by demand as demand profit pools do.

As we just saw with the dog food client, the Pampering Parents do, in fact, tend to be older empty nesters. But this does not by any means imply that all empty nesters with dogs are Pampering Parents. Nor does it mean that young singles, young families, or more mature families are never Pampering Parents; in fact, they often are. Indeed, Pampering Parents are a group of people defined by a common demand, not by common demographics. Although members of this group tend to skew to older empty-nester households, Pampering Parents will cut across almost all demographic groups.

Beyond a few tendencies, demographic segmentation offers little that's useful about the buying behavior of dog food purchasers. Not only isn't it enough, but what it does offer is usually also known to all of your competitors. In the end, demographic segmentation is very od at providing information about *who* your consumers are, but it rarely uncovers any critical information about *why* they are making those purchases.

One specific form of demographic market research is "firmographics." It's essentially a demographic approach used by business-to-business (B2B) industries to categorize their customers. In practice, firmographics creates profiles of business customers that typically relate to rough-cut industry vertical markets (manufacturing, retailing, financial services) and the size of the business (small, medium, large). If this reminds you of the early dog food business, you're not alone.

Firmographics is very popular. In recent years, we have worked with B2B clients around the world, in markets as diverse as medical devices, commercial printing, telecommunications, capital markets, and high technology, and nearly all of them were using this traditional industry vertical/size approach to try to understand the customers in their markets.

In almost every case, introducing the more sophisticated vision of demand profit pools, and the resulting demand landscape—that is, categorizing customers by *why* they make purchasing decisions—uncovers customers and opportunities these clients never knew existed, and they change their decision-making processes in response.

A bank we worked with provides a good example of the limitations of firmographics alone. This bank wanted to grow among small business customers, which often become much larger businesses over time, but was not having much success. Like many businesses, our client had segmented its potential small business banking clients into industry groups by size.

We quickly found that understanding the goals of each business (and the financing required to meet these goals) was a much more meaningful and actionable way to understand this market. Some of these businesses wanted to fuel aggressive growth, others had more moderate growth plans, and some were focused on preparing the business so it could be sold. Those small businesses that were family owned had other unique needs, including transitioning the business to the next generation or expanding the business to provide for multiple branches of the family.

Understanding these unique needs and the role financing played in each was the key this bank needed to unlock demand. Rather than calling on each business armed with fairly generic offers, the bank tailored its offers to the specific needs of each type of client.

Clients quickly took note. Discussions with this bank were suddenly much more meaningful because they focused on the clients' real demand, not just the fact that they happened to be in the retail, apparel, or construction businesses. And with offers that now reflected this new insight into clients' needs, the bank began winning significantly more small business clients.

Another traditional form of market segmentation is the behavioral approach—for example, "impulse magazine buyers." This technique assumes the decisions customers and consumers make today will be consistent with the choices and decisions they made yesterday.

Obviously, there is some value in this approach, because human beings are, generally speaking, consistent in their purchasing behavior. But this consistency is greatest during static periods—not, as today, during eras of rapid change and innovation. The behavioral approach again also sheds light only on *what* was purchased, not *why*.

Had we only examined who consumers were demographically, and what they were buying in the dog food marketplace, we would never have understood how significant an opportunity existed for our client. Nor could we have optimized the rest of the parent company's product portfolio by aligning with the distinctly different demands of each targeted demand profit pool. Instead, the market would most likely have continued to segment by size of dog and bagged or canned dog foods, thereby missing altogether the new demand opportunities we uncovered.

The net result of using a primarily behavior-focused approach is a bit like driving your car forward while only looking in the rearview mirror. Just because the road behind you was straight is no guarantee that the road ahead doesn't curve or come to a dead end. And a fast-moving, technology-driven world creates a lot of those curves and dead-ends: brand-new products and markets; existing businesses that suddenly become obsolete; the rapid proliferation of fads and fears carried by television, the Internet, and text messaging; and so on. And thanks to Moore's law and Metcalfe's law, this volatility is only going to increase in the years ahead, meaning that if you depend only on old information, you will not only be driving by looking in the rearview mirror, but putting your foot down ever more heavily on the accelerator.

If ever there was a time for looking through the front windshield, it is *now*.

UNDERSTANDING DECISIONS

Don't get us wrong: both demography and behavioral analysis are critical pieces of the puzzle in understanding demand. But in and of themselves they are insufficient. The data they generate must be put into the broader context of demand before they can be truly useful in segmenting markets.

The way companies can win in the new demand economy is by understanding how customers and consumers make decisions. Demand profit pools is the tool by which these companies first identify the most attractive customers and consumers and understand why they make the decisions they do. Starting immediately, companies can then take actions that align their products and services with the basis on which decisions are made. You know where consumer purchasing is going and how to get more of it, not just where it's been.

With a robust appreciation of demand profit pools, managers can construct profit and loss statements (P&Ls) pool by pool to track results. For example, in the dog food industry we just described, different companies might ask: *How much money are we making from* the Pampering Parents? Is there a way to increase the profitability of the Minimalist segment? How can we do a better job reaching the Performance Fuelers?

With a P&L segmented by demand profit pool, the finance team can better understand returns on investment and how to help improve them. The sales team can leverage the demand landscape to align the right offers with the right customers, dramatically increasing their odds of success.

As you might imagine, looking at one's business through the lens of demand profit pool analysis can be a truly eye-opening experience for a company and its management. It's not unusual for a company to discover that the group it thought contained its best and most-profitable customers is in fact populated by customers on whom the company *loses* money. Just as often, companies discover an extraordinarily attractive demand profit pool right before their eyes that they knew nothing about.

Once the demand profit pools have been developed, you can be certain they will evolve. You can track the change in two ways:

- *Qualitatively*, by talking with current customers or potential customers, or

- *Quantitatively*, using statistically valid survey techniques.

Either approach—or both in tandem—can yield insights not only into new and previously unknown profit pools, but also into determining those offering the most profit potential .

Even if you have not yet conducted a detailed analysis of your demand profit pools, you can get started in the right direction by identifying the top 10 percent heaviest spenders in your market, and then by asking: *What do these customers have in common? What is it that drives their decisions? What is the demand they are really trying to satisfy?*

Don't depend on your own answers to that question. Rather, invite that group in for an off-the-record, qualitative discussion about who they are and where they are going, what they really want from your company, and how well you are answering those needs. You will be amazed at how passionate they are about the category and how knowledgeable they are about your offerings—as well as the offerings of your competitors. We guarantee that you will learn a great deal from these "super consumers" about what you are doing right, what you are doing wrong, and what new opportunities are available to you that you may know nothing about. Most of all, you will ask yourself: *Why didn't we do this sooner?*

These super consumers and customers are not just to be found in a few industries. On the contrary, we have found them in almost every imaginable category—even in businesses in which the manufacturers serving them have long assumed their products have become all but forgotten commodities—things like office products, paper plates, soap, motor oil, and socks, just to name a few. What's more, in virtually every category we ever studied, the Pareto principle holds; that is, there is a strong 80/20 dynamic at work between super and regular customers. The super customers inevitably make up a small portion of the total customer population, but a significant portion of both spending and profits.[6]

That's why it's important to understand each demand profit pool individually—and by "understand" we don't mean a printout of monthly sales figures and the latest customer survey. No, you must *participate* in each demand profit pool—live it, understand it, and be able to describe not only the customers who populate it but what they want and how they make their purchasing decisions.

Here's an example: Say you are in the ice cream business. You will quickly find that there are people who love chocolate ice cream, those who prefer strawberry, and those who only eat vanilla. If you were to talk with all of them in a group, you'd come away convinced that the only way to succeed in the ice cream business is to exclusively manufacture Neapolitan ice cream. In truth, each of these flavors constitutes its own demand profit pool, with individual tastes (milk chocolate or dark chocolate) arrayed within them. And to simply aggregate past purchases to guide your strategy is to find yourself cornered in a small niche market.

A BETTER BEST BUY

We'll close this chapter with a case study that illustrates the difference between a demographic view of the marketplace and the demand profit pool strategy.

The company is Best Buy, one of the world's most successful retailers of electronic products and related services to consumers. The Minnesota-based company, founded in 1966 and with annual revenues of nearly $50 billion,[7] has had a storied history. What began as a single Sound of Music stereo shop now has more than 1,100 stores and 150,000 employees around the world.[8] Best Buy is also among the most honored of American businesses; it is regularly named one of the world's best specialty retailers as well as one of the nation's "most admired" companies.

Best Buy was also long considered a poster child for the power of "geodemographic market segmentation"—that is, segmenting customers by who they are, where they live, and what they've bought. The success Best Buy had with this strategy was the subject of a *Harvard Business Review* case study[9] and numerous magazine and newspaper articles. It was seen as the marketing model of the future and was imitated not only by competitors, but by companies in many other industries.

Best Buy's Customer Centricity approach identified several geodemographic segments of customers such as "young early adopter," "suburban mom," and "affluent customer." To bring these customer segments alive, Best Buy named each of them and developed detailed descriptions of each segment and their psyches. For example, the affluent customer was named Barry and he is described as a professional who wants the best technology and entertainment experience. Barry is generally over the age of thirty and is typically married. He is an achiever who strives to balance career and family. When it comes to electronics, Barry prefers the quality of premium brands and tends to be an early adopter of technology, especially when those technologies can offer him clear benefits. When it comes to an electronics retailer, Barry wants a store that provides a convenient, hassle-free shopping experience with end-to-end service.

Throughout 2004, Best Buy tested a new operating model based on this Customer Centricity in thirty-two U.S. lab stores.[10] This new operating model was designed to appeal specifically to the dominant customer segment or segments in a given store's neighborhood or "trading area." The sales associates, Best Buy's Blue Shirts, were trained specifically to understand and work with the customer segments dominant in their store. The store experience—including the product mix, product displays, merchandising, and of course service—were all tailored to the segment as well. Under Customer Centricity, a Best Buy store located in a wealthier white-collar suburb, for example, would be designed to appeal to Barry by focusing on premium brands, new but not necessarily cutting-edge technology, end-to-end service, and a hassle-free experience.

This approach proved to be a competitive breakthrough for Best Buy and the operating model tested in lab stores was rolled out to all U.S. stores. Customer Centricity not only enabled the company to identify key customer groups; it also allowed Best Buy to shrewdly locate those groups geographically and modify their stores in each trading area to match these variations in demand. Thus, there were Barry stores for the affluent customer, Buzz stores for young early adopters, and so on.

It was a highly effective strategy, and for a few years it paid off handsomely for Best Buy. But as we've already explained, demographic market segmentation—no matter how sophisticated the analysis, even when it includes a geographic dimension—has serious built-in limitations. The clearest and most powerful rearview mirror in the world is still, in the end, looking backward. And so by 2006, Best Buy management began to sense that the company had "hit a wall" in terms of the company's understanding of its customers' changing behaviors and preferences.

Prior to developing the new demand landscape, it had become apparent that:

- Best Buy's current geodemographic view of its customers was not generating new insights on their buying behavior.

- Traffic to the company's stores was slowing down.

- There was a perceived lack of differentiation between Best Buy and its competitors, and a growing concern about emerging low-cost competitors including Wal-Mart and Costco.

- The Best Buy brand had become ill defined and was losing its differentiation.

As Barry Judge, chief marketing officer of Best Buy recalled, "We were trying to develop an actionable segmentation approach to help us differentiate the brand, focus on the most important customers, and move our business forward. The demand landscape approach was very appealing to us. It really opened up the complete picture because it is very forward looking, brought many aspects of the customer together, is more robust, and makes the economic opportunities clear."[11]

We began our work with the Best Buy team by asking a series of questions:

1. Forces and Factors What are the current, latent, and emerging demands of consumers for technology and entertainment? What will influence how consumer demand evolves in the future?

2. Demand Profit Pools Which consumers carry the most profit and what is their unsatisfied demand?

3. How Can Best Buy Win? What is the compelling, differentiated value proposition that Best Buy will offer to its highest-profit customers in the future? What will be the value, in terms of revenues and profits, of this new strategy?

We began to look at the forces and factors at work on consumers of Best Buy's technology and entertainment (T&E) products and services, including computers, software, televisions, MP3 players, cameras, movies, games and game systems, smart phones, and appliances and the services to install, maintain, and repair them. Some of what we found is probably quite familiar. The average American family is busier than ever with work (often both parents are employed), school, organized activities, and the day-to-day of household chores. In previous generations, an extended family might have helped get everything done. But more often than not, today's extended families are spread out across the country or the world. Given how busy and how dispersed families are today, consumers have increasingly turned to technology to help manage the ways they live, learn, work, and play.

Smart phones, PCs, and cell phones help consumers stay connected with family, friends and co-workers at any time and from any place during their busy days. Grandma and grandpa might live across the country, but that doesn't mean they can't see their grandchild's first step, hear her first words, or share other moments that can be captured and streamed in real time. New technologies allow people to get work done more efficiently and with greater freedom to conduct that work while traveling. Or people can shift the office to the home by telecommuting. Consumers can spend their free time in new ways as well, from playing games online with others around the world, to finding almost any piece of music, to selecting from a nearly endless reservoir of movies and television programs to watch at any time.

Within this context, the team wanted to take our understanding of these consumers to a higher level. We wanted to understand more about the role electronics plays in people's lives—but more important, we wanted to understand their unfulfilled demands from technology. So we began talking with consumers about electronics, electronics retailers, the purchasing experience, and their own ongoing ownership experience. What we found was a significant disconnect between the demands of consumers and the supply-driven approaches of the electronics retailing industry, including our friends at Best Buy.

While retailers treated the electronics and technology sold in their stores as *products*, the most engaged consumers saw them as *enabling a lifestyle*. It was not the product per se that consumers were looking for. The real demand was for the more enriching experiences these products could potentially provide: staying connected with loved ones, capturing and sharing memories, unwinding together with games, movies or music, even getting schoolwork and office work done faster and better.

Consumers walked into the store with a vision of how technology could make work, school, free time, and life in general better, more fun, and more fulfilling. But far too often they walked out of electronics stores feeling intimidated and frustrated by all of the technical jargon thrown at them by salespeople, by the complexity of the choices available, by feeling pressured to buy, and by concerns about getting all of this great stuff up and running on their own once they got it home.

As we discussed our findings, the Best Buy team realized that there was a whole other layer of consumer demand that their geodemographic analysis had not uncovered. Together we recognized that we now had a signpost directing us toward previously undiscovered pools of demand. We now had a potential pathway from Best Buy's current demand to the latent demand just beginning to emerge.

To understand those high-profit pools of demand in more detail, we conducted our demand landscape analysis. It came up with equally compelling results. We identified five very different demand profit pools of consumers across the landscape. Here they are.[12]

Demand Segments Overview

Key Demand	Total	Enthusiasts	Online Aficionados	Practicals	Ambivalent Aspirers	Deal Drivens
		Love browsing, shopping for, and using products and services; prefer stores and tend to be less price-sensitive	Knowledgeable T&E experts and enthusiasts who prefer to purchase online; tend to be early adopters	Consumers who are comfortable with T&E but have only basic needs	Family-oriented consumers who have a love/hate relationship with T&E; often find T&E confusing	Price-conscious consumers who prefer to shop in-store; ability to return very important
% of Population	100%	16%	14%	27%	24%	19%
% of T&E Spend	100%	30%	25%	19%	16%	10%
Client Share of In-Store T&E Spend*	19%	22%	13%	21%	18%	20%
Client Share of Online T&E Spend*	5%	4%	15%	3%	3%	3%

Two of these demand profit pools immediately leapt out at us: the "Enthusiasts" and the "Online Aficionados." Together, they represented more than half of the spend category even though they were only about one-third of all consumers. These groups are always dreaming about a better home theater, an even cooler smart phone, a laptop, Net book, or iPad—the next mind-blowing technology that leaves others in the dust. They love new technologies and how they enrich their lives. Ronald Reagan once said "like most Americans, I live for the future,"[13] and clearly, Enthusiasts and Online Aficionados are the Americans who most live for, and furthest into, the future.

They are the most likely to be early adopters of technology and they are the most knowledgeable about the products they are buying. Unlike other consumers, these two groups will visit stores just to see what is new in T&E and will read about and research T&E not to make a purchase but simply to stay on top of what is going on. And given how important technology is to them, these two groups are by far the least price-sensitive.

On closer scrutiny, key differences between the two target groups emerged. The biggest of these was related to channel preferences. The

Online Aficionados, despite their appeal as early adopters of new technologies (and the higher margins those products usually bring), also tended to prefer buying items via the Web—indeed, they represented 55 percent of all online buying in this market[14]—and thus showed little loyalty to any particular retailer. These customers would surf the Web to find exactly what they wanted and while they frequently purchased from Amazon.com, they also felt comfortable purchasing products from a wide range of specialty online retailers focused solely on cameras or computers or almost any other product category. While Best Buy already had a comparatively sizable piece of the online T&E business, winning more business online—especially from Online Aficionados—would require a significant restructuring of Best Buy's online approach.

Enthusiasts were a very different story. This group was not only the most reliable customer for T&E, but also the biggest spender on those products—and most important, this group preferred shopping in electronics *stores*. When we looked at both traffic and spending, Enthusiasts had an impact (29 percent and 30 percent, respectively)[15] far beyond their actual share of the buying population (16 percent).[16] We now had our store target, the Enthusiasts, as well as an important target that used both the store and online but generally preferred to shop online, our Online Aficionados.

Other groups of consumers would be important contributors to sales for Best Buy as well, but for one reason or another they did not represent the highly profitable and highly attractive demand of Enthusiasts and Online Aficionados. Two of these other groups were relatively late adopters of technology who sat on the sidelines waiting for new technologies to become both more mainstream and more affordable. One, the "Practicals," had little or no emotional attachment to the T&E category but simply needed products like smart phones and PCs to be able to function in today's world. To some extent, they actually resented the fact that they were forced to adopt these technologies and got little or no pleasure from them. Another group, the "Ambivalent Aspirers," had a love/hate relationship with technology. They saw the value in technology, could even get excited about it, and aspired to master it. But members of this group felt that they did not have the technical skills to get these products up and running and to keep them functioning. In many cases, they relied on their teen or tween children to help them figure out the technology.

A final group, the "Deal Drivens," sought the benefits of technology but was motivated almost exclusively by the lowest prices, the biggest sales, and the best deals. For these, price was almost always the deciding factor in choosing where to purchase technology and what technologies to buy.

Clearly, Enthusiasts and Online Aficionados were the two most attractive groups to target and on which to focus Best Buy's efforts. It's important to remember that choosing a target to build your offers and your business around does not exclude the other segments of consumers who are not explicitly targeted. In our experience, the clarity of a well-defined and well-understood target helps managers create offers that are compelling to that target and often is also appealing to consumers within other demand profit pools. It should also be noted that what we had learned about the new demand profit pools only added to the existing Customer Centricity geodemographic approach, rather than replacing it.

By making itself the destination of choice for the most discerning Enthusiasts and Online Aficionados, Best Buy gained important credibility and perceived expertise that made it attractive to consumers outside of the target as well. By deeply understanding their targets and having the sophisticated products and experienced Blue Shirt sales staff and Geek Squad technical support who could answer the tough questions these knowledgeable consumers had, Best Buy was creating an experience that was also attractive to other consumers. The halo of expertise and credibility Best Buy built was attractive even to consumers who sought out less-than-cutting-edge technology. Consumers outside of the target would often say, "I know Best Buy has really knowledgeable salespeople and a wide range of products. I don't need the latest and greatest technology, but they will help me find exactly what I need and they will deliver and install it if I want them to."

Best Buy's targeted demand profit pools represented the potential consumers who could put the company back on its historic pace. We even knew that the consumers' underlying demand from technology was for more enriching experiences. But what exactly did that mean—and how could Best Buy turn that desire into actual demand for products and services?

We decided to deconstruct these enriching experiences into a distinct set of "usage occasions" or need states for technology—and then see, via interviews and surveys, if we could attach a dollar value to each. Recall from our earlier discussion that need states reflect how the choices made by a group of consumers will change depending on the situation or the occasion. One of the first applications of need states was for Gatorade and the "hot and sweaty" need state Gatorade was so perfectly aligned with.[17]

Let us share three of the many usage occasions—the "need states" we identified:

Need States for Best Buy

Need State	Description	Importance	Spend
Fun-Filled Free Time	➤ Getting the most from my free time by enjoying my favorite entertainment, hobbies, and passions	Highest	Highest
Celebrations	➤ Making all of the special events in my life truly special with the right gifts, music, and photos, and being able to capture and share these events	High	Moderate
Always in Touch	➤ Being in touch with family, friends, and co-workers, and getting the information I need whenever I want to be	High	Higher

Not surprisingly, one of the biggest usage occasions for T&E is focused on fun. One of the reasons so many consumers love T&E products is that they can make free time more fun by enabling them to play games, engage in hobbies such as photography, indulge in a passion such as music, follow a favorite sports team, or just kick back with a movie. Another key usage occasion had to do with the many special occasions we celebrate throughout the year. From sending a gift card for a birthday, to hosting an elaborate party, the T&E category can provide the gifts, music, videos, and games as well as the cameras to record every moment. A final example had to do with the need to be in touch with other people and the information—phone numbers, addresses, driving directions—people need whenever they need them.

The message was clear: for Best Buy to fulfill the demands of the Enthusiasts, it would need to create a unique store environment in which knowledgeable and friendly employees would guide those Enthusiasts through the *experience* of a new technology or product, help them put together the right package of products to achieve a *solution* tailored for their needs, and then follow up to make sure that this system was installed properly and delivering the enriching experiences Enthusiasts were seeking.

As Brian Dunn, new CEO of Best Buy, told the press as his new role was announced in January 2009, at the height of the economic uncertainty surrounding the recession, "We continue to be in uncharted economic waters, but one thing is certain: Our strategy remains unchanged. That strategy is to focus [on] customers and enrich their lives with the products Best Buy sells, empowering them with technology."[18]

To deliver on its strategy, Best Buy implemented the following actions:

- Training its Blue Shirts to be certified product experts

- Creating in-store demonstration areas where consumers could try products

- Having products available and in stock for immediate purchase more often

- Providing assistance (through Best Buy's Geek Squad) for delivering products, setting them up, and resolving any problems

- Reaching across all twenty-eight of its departments in both its stores and its online site to determine how to more closely align its offerings, services, and customer experience to match the demands of the Enthusiasts and Online Aficionados

Needless to say, all of this training, improvement, and added inventory was a significant investment. Would it pay off for Best Buy?

As we worked across categories in the store and online, we found that the new insights into Enthusiasts and Online Aficionados provided a much deeper understanding of Best Buy's most important customers, how they made decisions in the T&E category, and how the company could win with them. By viewing each category from the perspective of Enthusiasts and Online Aficionados, the team identified significant new opportunities for profitable growth.

One such opportunity related to the mobile devices—cell phones and smart phones—that are so critical to the "Always in Touch" need state. The opportunity for Best Buy to create a unique experience and to win in mobile devices was so large, it had the potential to multiply Best Buy's share in this critical category. As *The Wall Street Journal* reported, Best Buy "now believes that it can quintuple its share of the U.S. mobile-phone market to 15 percent."[19] Dunn and his team were so confident that they could leverage the new insights into explosive growth, he set the expectations for it with analysts on Wall Street and in the press.

Another example, aimed at the Online Aficionados, was a major overhaul of Best Buy's online approach and the bestbuy.com Web site. Improvements included customer reviews, product comparisons, help finding the right product for your needs, clicking to have a representative call to answer your question, ordering online for store pickup, and more. The result of all of these improvements has been to rapidly more than double online sales.

According to Best Buy CMO Judge, "The new insights really helped us differentiate from competition by determining where to invest behind new benefits and at what level of investment. The economics were so clear, they allowed marketing to really talk to all of the other functions across the organization using the language everyone speaks: the bottom line."[20]

As we write this, the transformation of Best Buy is not only still underway—for the fourth quarter of 2009, revenues increased 12.4 percent and profits jumped 37 percent from the year before[21] and Best Buy has gained three share points[22]—but this strategy has also begun to drive highly profitable new services to empower Best Buy customers to get the most from their technology purchases. And it has guided Best Buy into new product categories outside its traditional focus on technology and entertainment, such as guitars and musical instruments, that can further enrich the lives of customers.

What began as a simple concern at Best Buy to understand customer demand at a deeper level has helped lead a major transformation of the entire consumer electronics industry.

———

As you've seen, once Best Buy understood it was not just selling products but was actually enriching the lives of consumers, it opened up whole new ways to compete and win. The fact is, once you understand demand, you are then able to shape and differentiate your supply so it better satisfies the highest-profit demand for your products or services. The starting point is to develop the depth of understanding that goes far beyond typical segmentation approaches. To do that will require a level of precision that is all but unprecedented in measuring demand. The good news is even that is now possible—as you'll see in the next chapter.

THE FIFTH *P*

*Bringing a New Level of
Precision to Your Business*

In the new demand economy, the margin for error for all businesses grows smaller and smaller.

In the flagrantly expansionary economy of the past several years, sloppiness in planning and execution were hidden as business sales and profits went up constantly. These days, you are not only competing with ever growing sources of supply from competitors all over the world, but all of that supply is competing for flattening—even contracting—demand. In this new competitive reality, *any* mistake can have significant consequences.

The solution must go beyond tightening the screws still further on the supply chain. Now, the precision must occur on the demand side of the equation.

One reason for this is a shift in expectations. Today's customers and consumers expect more precision from business because, thanks to the tech revolution, the world around us has become much more precise. GPS devices will show you within inches how to get from point A to point B. Atomic clocks measure to the billionths of seconds. Twitter can tell you exactly what your friends are up to at any given moment. YouTube, TiVo, and iTunes allow you to access the history of recorded entertainment to find exactly the experience you want at that moment. And cellular telephony lets people contact you anywhere on the globe.

In the face of this unprecedented increase in precision, is it any wonder that customers and consumers are increasingly impatient with inaccuracies, delays, and imprecision? Precision has become the leitmotif of the lives of your consumers—and if you fail to match that precision, those failings will seem even more amplified.

What consumers also instinctively understand is that precision has long been a precursor of progress. In high technology, ever smaller chips also have ever more functionality. In medicine, laparoscopic and laser surgery enables doctors to work in small, almost microscopic, spaces instead of using more invasive procedures. Heart stents are implanted with precision to prevent heart attacks and strokes. The Kindle delivers thousands of books to your home on a small device within seconds, and soon tiny chips called RFID (for radio frequency identification) will track individual packages as they travel across America or around the world. Precision is almost always the path into the future.

———

We have seen similar shifts in expectations in the past. Twenty years ago, we experienced a shift to immediacy, to a 24/7 world, thanks to the Internet and companies such as Federal Express and Amazon. More recently, mobility has become an everyday expectation, enabled again by the Internet, by telepresence and technologies such as Skype and Second Life, and driven by a natural desire among people to stay connected with each other wherever they are.

The biggest corporate success story of the century to date, Google, is perhaps the perfect exemplar of the growing need for—and the power of—precision. As consumers, most of us would be lost trying to find what we need on the Internet without Google or another search engine. But acting as a tool to help you find precisely what you are looking for on the Web only explains in part what has made Google such an amazing game changer.

The real power of Google is its ability to help advertisers increase the efficiency and effectiveness of their advertising spending through greater precision. The company helps advertisers reach exactly those consumers who are most likely to be interested in their message. Indeed, almost every significant purchase (as well as many smaller purchases) consumers make today begins with online research. Consumers have learned to compare hotels, cars, TVs, shoes, and a thousand other product categories via the Web. What's more, the consumers conducting these searches are much more likely than the average TV viewer, newspaper reader, or radio listener to actually make a purchase in the category being researched.

The genius of Google's business strategy is that it placed itself right in the middle of this research/decision-making process—an idea so radical that it caught potential competitors, such as the big newspaper and magazine families, so completely by surprise that they not only cheered the rise of Google, but often even turned over their Web page to the Google search engine. By the time the media giants realized their mistake, Google had placed itself at the crossroads of the online retail and advertising world.

In practice, Google can show its advertiser clients precisely how consumers who saw their advertisements online actually behave. Google can also show how many consumers actually click on an ad or visit an advertiser's site for additional information. The advertisers in turn can see the increase in traffic to their site, as well as where this traffic came from, time spent on the site, pages viewed, and, of course, *sales*.

SEARCHING FOR PROFITS

Like Google, adding greater precision to your business model has the potential to turn it into a kind of "profit search engine" that can be used to pinpoint the most profitable demand in a market, to help you understand the basis for decision making of those customers, and help align your supply precisely with the highest-profit demand.

Injecting greater precision into your business model drives both greater efficiency and greater effectiveness. And Google isn't the only company that has come to appreciate that fact.

Consider the case of gaming-resort giant Harrah's.

Harrah's, founded in 1937, is currently the world's largest gaming corporation,[1] due in large part to the efforts of its current chairman and CEO, Gary Loveman, who joined the company in 1998[2] with the intention of taking the gamble out of the gambling business. Loveman has made a career out of precision. Prior to joining Harrah's, he was a professor at Harvard Business School and had spent two years at the Federal Reserve Bank in Boston performing regression analysis research on the U.S. budget deficit.

Loveman's innovative strategy consisted of four parts, all targeted at identifying the most profitable demand pools (which largely turned out to be average gamblers instead of the usual "high rollers"), learning about them, and then tying them as closely as possible to the Harrah's experience. Loveman turned precision into profits, much as you can do. Here are the four parts of the strategy:[3]

• *Total Rewards* A four-tiered customer loyalty program that begins with Gold at the entry level and progresses to Platinum, Diamond, and Seven Stars, based on a customer's level of play. Platinum, Diamond, and Seven Stars cardholders receive progressively greater levels of service, which adds an aspirational element to the program. To increase membership, the card is also quite easy to sign up for, easy to use, capable of accruing credits from any Harrah's property, and can be used for rewards at various company resorts. Critical to Total Rewards is upward mobility; customers are motivated to move up in the plan through increasing benefits with increasing participation.

• *Demand Pools* These four tiers of customers, as defined by the Total Rewards program, are further segmented into about ninety customer groups based on their geodemographics, psychographics, and play patterns.[4] This information is then used to predict each player's frequency and financial value in the future. Player data are constantly upgraded and fine tuned to stay abreast of any changes in the market-place in order to adjust strategy accordingly. For example, based on slot customers' actual wins and losses, visit frequency, play denomina-tions, and velocity, Harrah's can identify the profitability of classes of customers.[5] In one case, based on this information, Harrah's decided to consolidate its strategy around "avid experience players," middle-aged folks with the time and discretionary income who gamble $100 to $500 a trip and visit Harrah's properties several times a year.[6] This fact-based and precise understanding of Harrah's most profitable cus-tomers is a very far cry from their competitors, who lavished attention on a small number of wealthy players.

• **Real-Time Data** This constant scanning for changes in the business environment, combined with analysis of customer data, gives Harrah's a clear advantage over its competitors. Any deviations or changes in predominant customer taste or behavior is immediately picked up by the system, and the company can then rapidly adapt its strategy to match the changed circumstances.

• **Direct Mail** Harrah's sends out nearly 250 million nonacquisition pieces of direct mail per year, along with nearly 8 million e-mails per month on the Internet and thousands of telephone calls to communi-cate with its various segments.[7] Surveys have found that card members actually look forward to deals from Harrah's. The response rate for such offers by Harrah's averages about 10 percent, five times that of the industry average.[8]

Using all of these tools, Harrah's has built a precise operating system based on a proprietary understanding of demand. The company uses this system to find, reward, and create loyalty among their most profit-able customers.

The results of this four-prong, demand-oriented precision strategy have been both sweeping and consequential. The program has driven revenue increases across all of Harrah's properties, with its Las Vegas properties in particular experiencing double-digit growth.[9] This growth has been matched by a growing mindshare of Harrah's target customers: gaming by customers who use their Rewards cards jumped by nearly 6 percent, while in just a decade, Harrah's share of customer gaming budgets grew by 10 percent, to 45 percent today.[10]

Most remarkably, all of this success was achieved even as Harrah's cut its ad spending by nearly half.[11] Today, thanks in large part to its Rewards program, and the sophisticated customer analysis tools that accompany it, nearly 50 percent of Harrah's revenues is driven by direct marketing.[12] Under Loveman, Harrah's knows its customers, understands their demand, knows their gaming habits, and knows how to capture more of their gaming expenditures.

Clearly, Harrah's is no longer just rolling the dice on its business planning.

THE NEW MARKETING MIX

Supply chain management became a science through the creation of more rigorous approaches that increased quality, reduced costs, and shrank production cycle time. Every aspect of what before had been the siloed functions of purchasing, manufacturing, and distribution was now assessed, optimized, and interlinked using several fact-based approaches.

Today, an equally rigorous approach to demand is both necessary and practical. It needs to be done and it can be done. And the initiatives undertaken during the supply chain revolution, as described above, can serve as guideposts to what can be done now to transform demand.

So too can another, equally famous set of principles help us to find our way. The marketing mix is best known as the "four *P*'s of marketing": product, promotion, place, and price. If we apply the philosophy of precision to this mix, the potential benefits become enormous.

• **Product** Only a fraction of the more than $1 trillion invested each year by U.S. corporations in innovation[13] actually results in successful innovation. The rest—hundreds of billions of dollars that could be put to more productive use—is written off.

• **Promotion** As retail magnate John Wanamaker famously noted, "Half the money I spend on advertising is wasted; the trouble is I don't know which half."[14] Unfortunately, this is as true today as when Wanamaker made this quip more than a century ago.

• **Place** Recent estimates calculate that U.S. manufacturers lose a staggering $93 billion per year due to out-of-stock items at retail locations.[15] That's prequalified, ready-to-buy consumers who have to be turned away because the items are unavailable.

• **Price** As we've already noted, pricing power for the period from 1991 to 2009, as compared to the period from 1947 to 1990, declined 79 percent in business-to-business (B2B) markets, while in business-to-consumer (B2C) markets it declined by 35 percent.[16]

These are just some of the most glaring examples of the tremendous financial penalties imposed by a lack of precision. Given these huge sums and the potential prize to anyone who can overcome these errors, one has to ask two questions: *Why haven't we addressed this sooner?* and *Where do we start?*

It is time for the adoption of a fifth *P,* precision, to make sure that each of the first four *P*'s operate at their maximum efficiency and lowest cost. A lot of companies have already noticed; Coca-Cola, for example, has already declared this "the Age of Precision Marketing."[17]

Precision couldn't come at a more important moment.

Retailers are becoming much more precise in terms of what they really need in their stores to serve their consumers. As a result, retailers are dramatically cutting back on the SKUs they carry.[18] Store chains are effectively saying: "We don't need fifteen configurations of tissues. Our customers don't want that much complexity in their decision making. We'll cut back to five types of tissues—and make two of them private labels of our own."

Retailers are also being more precise about how many stores they need and where they should be located. Recently this has led to a wave of store closings—too many retailers overextended their stores during the last boom and now they are racing to retrench. There are simply too many "doors" to serve a flattening GDP.

The result is a dangerous nexus: a convergence of consumers expecting more precision in their lives, retailers cutting back on product diversity, and manufacturers increasingly needing to match their supplies with flattened or shrinking demand. And yet most companies remain unaware that any of this is going on around them.

KNOW THYSELF

If you want to determine where your own company falls on the continuum between being supply driven versus demand driven, between being error prone and precision driven, take a moment to answer the following eleven questions:

1. How precise is your customer targeting across your portfolio of brands?

2. Will customer targeting based on demographics, geodemographics, or industry verticals alone be precise enough for you to win?

3. Precisely which of your customer targets creates the most net profit for your business?

4. How precise is your understanding of which media deliver what results, and what the right mix of media is to deliver the best total results?

5. How precise are you at getting the right product to the right store, at the right time, in the right pack size?

6. How precise are you at allocating spending geographically so that your budget is precisely aligned with where the most profit can be made?

7. How precise are you at allocating resources to your highest potential growth businesses?

8. How precise are you at determining the potential financial success of innovation opportunities before you commit and spend the money to bring your new ideas to market?

9. Are you certain that your training programs provide the precision required to equip your managers to understand and master even the most difficult situations in their new assignments?

10. How precise are your two- and three-year growth plans to achieve the profits expected by shareholders?

11. How precise are you in your pricing strategy?

That's a beginning. It is also possible to create a supplemental list of questions that focuses on the unique characteristics of a specific industry or category. For example, here are some precision questions that might be asked in the retail world:

1. How precise are your operations at each of your retail locations? Do you have one operating manual, or do you create more precision at different locations and at stores that have different configurations?

2. How precise are you at understanding the strategic roles different categories of products play in your store?

3. How precisely do you know which discounts provide the highest volume and profit?

Today, few companies can answer all of these questions with any degree of precision. Indeed, it is likely that as you read the questions, you had to answer some of them with "I don't know" or, at best, with "Pretty good, I think," with little empirical evidence to back up that claim. That won't be true a few years from now: in the current global economic climate, if by then you can't answer all of these questions with either "Excellent" or with a precise metric, you will have a serious, profit-threatening problem on your hands.

MARKETING TOOL KIT

So these are the challenges, the questions that your competitors are starting to try to answer. And here are some of the new solutions.

One of the best ways to bring greater precision and rigor to many businesses is to systematically study how to allocate resources. Ultimately, making resource allocation decisions in order to achieve corporate objectives is the fundamental job of every manager, from brand managers to division managers to country managers to the CEO. Unfortunately, far too often these critical decisions are made based on past precedent rather than future potential. This hidebound approach becomes entrenched as "the way we've always done it" and resists any attempt at change regardless of potential opportunities.

Inevitably, the result is that the business or brand that has always been allocated at 10 percent of available resources continues to get 10 percent of available resources, whether it deserves it (or perhaps more) or not. In the worst cases, resource allocation goes to the manager who argues the most persuasively, whether this makes strategic sense or not.

The connection between understanding demand and precisely targeting that demand with the right resources ultimately produces better decisions, a better resource allocation process, and ultimately, more profit. Building on the tools we introduced in Chapter 3—demand landscapes and the demand profit pools—we've also developed an additional methodology that helps a company precisely align each of its businesses and brands with its highest potential opportunities. Moreover, each brand or business can also be assessed both in terms of their absolute market potential and in relation to each other. We call it the "portfolio matrix."

Now that you understand the demand profit pools for your market and the specific demands of each, the next logical question is how to allocate your resources to capture the highest possible share of profitable demand. Not surprisingly, the portfolio matrix adds a new level of precision to your resource allocations. Here's an example:

Example Portfolio Matrix

	Brand Growth Potential	
High (Brand Economics)	**Protect and Maintain** ➤ Anchors the Business System − Significant scale and profitability − Flat to moderately declining growth	**Fuel Strategic Growth Engines** ➤ Drives Near-Term Profit Growth − Significant scale and profitability − Positive growth trend with significant remaining upside − High strategic value
(Brand Economics)	**Manage for Margin** ➤ Funds High Potential Brands − Moderate scale and profitability − Flat to declining growth trend	**Build High Potential Brands** ➤ Drives Medium-Term Profit Growth − Proven alignment with demand landscape and demonstrated growth momentum − High potential for national scale and above-average margins
Low (Brand Economics)	**Divest** ➤ Removes Financial & Opportunity Costs − Small scale and declining growth − Negative to below average variable and selling margins	**Learn and Prove** ➤ Drives Medium- to Long-Term Growth − Potential alignment with the demand landscape − Unproven scale/economics
	Low ——— Brand Growth Potential ——— **High**	

This simple two-by-three matrix yields six strategic roles each business or brand can play within the portfolio—as well as the different resource allocation levels and actions (the inner squares) to take for each of those six roles. As you can see, these roles range from a business or brand with low growth potential and poor economics (a likely candidate for divestiture) to those that have high growth potential and highly attractive economics that represent strategic growth opportunities.

The portfolio matrix works because it abandons past prejudices and instead throws a company's real business into high relief. It makes for a perfect starting point for infusing greater precision throughout the company. Properly applied, the matrix changes how resource allocation is done at most companies. Using the matrix, businesses are aligned based on their future capability to grow and produce profits. In effect, it is a vertical arrangement, with the highest-growth businesses at the top, and slow-growth businesses at the bottom.

The process we follow with the matrix is to first determine precisely how much of our pool of resources is required to fund the three boxes on the right side of the matrix, where most future growth comes from. We next allocate sufficient resources to ensure that the large slow-growth businesses in the box at upper left are able to contribute the profitability expected from them.

Finally, we come to the last two boxes, at the lower left. We frequently find that there are few resources to devote to these boxes. They are then allocated few resources, or are tagged to be sold or shut down. It is the precise discipline used in this two-by-three portfolio matrix tool that ensures that the right level of resources is given to the future growth engines. This is the technique used by many of the company case examples described throughout this book to win the most profitable demand in the market by aligning resources with opportunities.

Beyond the landscape and the portfolio matrix, several other tools are available to enhance precision in a company's operations. We'll briefly describe each of them—demand gap analysis, customer demand analysis, and predictive modeling analysis—and then show how they were put to use in that most American of product categories: hot dogs.

Demand Gaps

Formally speaking, demand gap analysis is a form of econometric analysis used to identify the most significant gaps between those benefits and features being offered by an industry's current products and services and the ideal sought by each demand profit pool of customers.

In practice, demand gaps are really quite simple: they are the distance between what your customer wants and what it gets from you or your competitors.

It used to be that you asked consumers for a description of that gap—that is, what consumers saw as important, and what none of your competitors did well. Then faced with, say, five opportunities—the reality being that you couldn't do them all—you were forced to guess. This led to a lot of wasted investments and a few disasters (Delta's Song air service, the Ford Edsel, the IBM PCjr), but most companies survived. Today, the consequences of such failures are much greater. You now need a much more rigorous process than intuition and your gut feel to determine which of those demand gaps is the most valuable.

Needless to say, this decision process is the perfect place in which to apply precision tools. And modern demand gap analysis has just such a tool: derived importance. It starts with those gaps consumers tell you about, then uses rigorous analytic processes to enable you to tell which of those four or five gaps, when closed, will return the greatest revenues and profits. In a remarkable and financially precise way, derived importance takes the guesswork out of the decision making when it comes to choosing which demand gap opportunity to pursue.

Managers are often astonished by the results of demand gap analysis. Why? Because most of them had only seen the broadest metrics, often just customer satisfaction scores or related assessments that include all consumers and aggregate back to the mean. By comparison, demand gap analysis provides—often for the first time—three incredibly valuable new insights:

- An understanding of gaps from the perspective of targeted demand profit pools

- The ranking of benefits and features that those demand pools find most and least important

- The economic value of addressing those gaps

The example below is a demand gap analysis for the credit card industry. The first chart is the result of asking several thousand target consumers what benefits they find most important from a credit card. As you can see, consumers thought a company that was "On my side" was most important and that "Fraud prevention" was the next most important benefit.

Once consumers told us what benefits were most important, we then had them rate the performance of competitors in the industry and of our client for each benefit. This gave us a performance score for the industry on average (and we had the details for each competitor) as well as for our client. You can see that many of the biggest gaps between importance and performance are for some of the benefits consumers value most. For our client, some of the areas where they outperformed the industry still showed significant gaps, from the consumer's perspective. These gaps provide some interesting hypotheses for potential areas of improvement. However, there was more analysis to do before taking action to close any of these gaps.

Demand Gaps (Industry Underperformance) for Credit Cards

Need Statement	Importance	Competitor Performance	Client Performance	Industry Performance Gap	Client Performance Gap	
On my side	77%	22%	18%	−55%	−59%	
Fraud prevention	72	21	22	−51	−50	← *While client outperforms competitors on important security-related needs, it falls well short of consumer expectations*
No hidden charges	67	33	21	−34	−46	
Lowest interest rate	66	15	9	−51	−57	
Purchase protection	55	33	34	−22	−21	←
Lowest annual fee	53	24	16	−29	−37	
Quick issue resolution	51	25	16	−26	−35	
Appreciates me	44	16	15	−28	−29	
Extended warranties	43	16	18	−27	−25	
ATM fees	42	17	10	−25	−32	

The next set of analyses we conducted with these data determined the derived importance of each of the benefits that consumers had stated as important. Unlike stated importance, derived importance is a statistical approach that correlates a known behavior with the factors that led to it. In this case, the known behavior was credit card ownership. Of all of the benefits consumers stated as important, derived importance determined which benefits were most highly correlated with credit card ownership.

In other words, derived importance determined the benefits that are actually most linked to owning a credit card or a certain type of credit card. In effect, the analysis identified benefits that were critical to the decision to own a credit card—benefits that consumers might not even be capable of articulating. As behavioral economics has shown, consumer decision making is not always rational. But as consumers review a list of credit card benefits in a survey, they may try to act in a more rational way than they do in the real world.

So while "On my side" seemed important, the more tangible benefit of "Purchase protection" proved to be a more important driver of actual credit card ownership for this group of consumers. The implication was that this credit card company could win more business with this group of consumers if it could reduce or close the gap in performance on "Purchase protection" and make consumers aware of this. But how much should they invest to do so?

To answer that question, we assessed the economic value (in terms of revenue gains in millions of U.S. dollars) to improving the performance on each benefit. We determined the economic upside of improving performance from current levels by 5 percent up to a 25 percent improvement. Now our client could determine where to invest, based on the cost associated with improving each benefit area and the upside available from doing so.

Opportunity Summary – Value of Addressing Demand Gaps (US$, Millions)

	Derived Importance	5%	10%	15%	20%	25%
Security	Purchase protection	$38	$76	$114	$155	$193
	Extended warranty	19	39	58	78	97
	Fraud prevention	15	31	50	66	88
Advocacy	Quick issue resolution	29	54	86	112	141
	On my side	22	45	71	89	111
	Appreciates me	12	25	40	55	66
Fees	ATM fees	17	40	56	82	99
	Lowest annual fee	12	24	36	47	57
	Lowest interest rate	10	21	30	39	46
Transparency	No hidden charges	21	41	62	82	103
	Country-specific drivers	*67*	*131*	*206*	*281*	*323*
	Total	**$262**	**$527**	**$809**	**$1,086**	**$1,324**

Customer Demand Analysis

One of the most important decisions business managers have to make regards business strategy. It is also one of the most difficult because there are typically many apparently good options for a strategy.

In a typical scenario, senior managers come together, discuss the circumstances, share their experiences, and make strategic decisions. But nowadays, there's too much at stake for such a purely subjective process—thus the rise of new tools to help quantify those key alternative strategies.

We call this "Customer Demand Analysis." It is designed to determine first who the most profitable customers are for your business. The second step is to actually contact those customers and, through a series of interactions, empower them to determine for you precisely the business proposition they want, the message that will work best to motivate them, the price they are willing to pay, the media through which you'll find them, and the best channel to reach them. In other words, they provide you with the blueprint for the strategy you will use to grow your business.

Meanwhile, along the way, these customers will also provide you with valuable insights into the vulnerabilities of your most important competitors. After all, who would know them better?

Acting as a manager's dashboard, customer demand analysis enables you to quantitatively build a pro forma profit and loss statement, predict what your revenues will be, and lets your business and finance team determine levels of profitability.

There is one final, less tangible but no less important benefit as well. Because you are doing all of this work with your most profitable demand pools, you are all but assured of both their continued loyalty and increased business with them. Conversely, you don't waste money on something that won't work and risk either hurting your brand or giving your competitor a chance to grow at your expense.

In practice, the most obvious and immediate impact of customer demand analysis is in helping to define the value-added features (that is, customer desired *and* profit generating) of your products. Thus, if it's food, you'll learn what should it taste like; if clothing, what style it should be? By the same token, it prevents you from bolting on features and applications that look popular but ultimately that will only cost you money.

Credit cards provide a classic example of this. If you remember, years ago the major credit cards had long lists of features, such as emergency medical assistance. Many of these added services were quite costly to maintain, but it was assumed that they were critical to the appeal of these credit cards. Yet in real life, consumers rarely took advantage of these features. Ultimately, surveys found that not only did most cardholders not even know they existed, but once they learned about them, had little need for them anyway. The credit card company quietly dropped those add-ons and focused instead on those things that consumers really wanted: greater access, better service, lower interest rates.

As with demand gaps, managers are almost always surprised by the priority of benefits and features that are most—and least—valued by customers in their key demand profit pools, as well as the overall impact on value from each of those benefits/features. One of the most consistent findings from this analysis is what can be characterized as the "don't hide your light under a bushel" syndrome. Customer Demand Analysis almost always reveals the power of a few key benefits and features that the product or service already delivers—but of which customers in the most attractive demand profit pools are largely unaware. These opportunities are especially valuable because they can be acted on almost immediately as they are already part of the offering. In other words, they can be a quick way to turn big profits.

Predictive Modeling

Now that product and service offers have been precisely optimized to target the best demand profit pools, you still need to reach those customers with your message. Predictive modeling and "microtargeting" are used to precisely reach the targeted audience with the right message. When done correctly, these tools can dramatically increase the efficiency and effectiveness of the advertising and marketing communications spend.

Predictive modeling uses statistical analysis to determine to which demand profit pool a given customer is likely to belong—and to do so with a high degree of accuracy, often in excess of 80 percent. Predictive modeling can be applied to a company's existing customer list to determine which distinct demand profit pools thousands or even millions of customers are in. It can also be applied to data related to prospective customers to determine which demand profit pools they fall into, and therefore which offers these prospective customers should receive. Traditionally, this approach has been used by companies that enjoy a direct relationship with their customers, such as banks, credit card issuers, telecommunications providers, and retailers. By identifying and reaching customers by their demand profit pool, these businesses are now able to send offers specifically tailored to those groups—microtargeting them—by electronic or direct mail.

Increasingly, even businesses that do not have direct relationships with their customers are leveraging the power of predictive modeling to microtarget. They are doing so with the new generation of Web 2.0 and social media tools such as Facebook and Twitter, and by taking advantage of the growing number of mobile devices. This microtargeting enables businesses to narrowcast to a small group of customers—even individuals—with a tailored message or offer. So precise has this narrowcasting become that via Twitter, small bakeries and coffee shops in New York City and Silicon Valley now offer sales to regular customers that last only a few minutes—or to notify them of an available table, or tell them that the bread is just coming out of the oven.

SPEAKING FRANKLY

To show the power of precision—working through the full portfolio of analytical tools—not only to reshape a company's business, but to keep it in a hugely profitable business it was prepared to deemphasize, let's look at the story of Ball Park Franks.

Since its founding in 1957,[19] Ball Park Franks has enjoyed both business and pop culture ("Plump when you cook them!") success. But even after being purchased by Sara Lee in 1989,[20] the company still struggled as the number two player[21] in the $1.7 billion hot dog category.[22] As the company entered the new century, it faced flat growth and seemed unable to make a dent in the strong franchise the number one brand had built in the category. At one point, Ball Park even considered focusing on other markets, such as sausages, where it thought it could win, instead of essentially settling for being a distant number-two player in the hot dog market.

Beginning in 2005, Ball Park was focused on a strategy of mass marketing to adult males during the summer grilling season.[23] In this strategy, any appreciable new growth would come from moving into similar, adjacent markets or through specialized packaging ("singles"), and sales would be supported through additional national trade spending. In other words, pretty much the same thing the company had always done—just more of it. It was not a new approach, and by targeting all adult males it was not a very precise approach. As such, it was not the source of much optimism either inside the company or among their retail customers . . . and, in fact, the results were disappointing.

That's when we began working with Ball Park to determine if a more precise, demand-driven analysis of the market could identify profitable new growth opportunities.

The first step was to look at the company's target market. It seemed self-evident that the biggest market for hot dogs probably was adult males during the summer barbecue season. But was it really true?

In fact it was—but the size of this market segment was nowhere near what Ball Park thought it was. In reality, summer grilling consumers represented just 30 percent of the total hot dog business.[24] So we took the question apart and asked two different questions:

1. Who are the other major consumers of hot dogs?

2. Is there another time of year when hot dogs sell well—perhaps a year-round market?

As it turned out, we discovered a vast new year-round market sitting out there that was all but unaddressed by Ball Park or any of its competitors. It was those voracious eating machines known as teen and 'tween' boys.

It was one of those "Well, of course!" moments that confirm what was always right before our eyes but never affirmed.

Further research underscored something we always knew and something else we always suspected: teenage boys eat massive amounts of food, basically on a continual basis—and they will satisfy their hunger with anything at hand, especially junk food. And in an era when both mom and dad are likely to be working, many of these hungry teenagers come home from school to an empty house and have only a brief interval, typically an hour, to fuel up before heading off to afterschool sports, band, or other activities.

Meanwhile, our research confirmed, the mothers of these boys are very concerned about the nutritional value and healthfulness of the afterschool snacks their boys are consuming—but being absent, they have little control over the selection process. Thus, these moms, who typically do the food shopping for the household, are in a perpetual search for snack items that are both healthful *and* have a high likelihood of being voluntarily selected by their sons.

So now we had an untapped potential market and the beginnings of an understanding of how the players in that market behaved—as well as their roles in purchasing and consumption. But we still didn't understand the *attitudes* and *decision criteria* of those players, and what role they might play in promoting or impeding the sale of Ball Park Franks in that market.

Here's what further research found: like many Americans, the mothers of those teenage boys had a lot of misconceptions about hot dogs, most notably about their ingredients. Adult men, sitting at a baseball game or cooking on the barbecue, don't really care about ingredients, but moms do, especially for their children.

So the first branding challenge was obviously to correct those misperceptions by stressing the *actual* ingredients in a Ball Park hot dog. Our surveys found that moms felt much better about all-beef hot dogs than they did about regular hot dogs. Beef hot dogs were always part of Ball Park's portfolio but were now made the focus. The "made with 100 percent beef" emphasis immediately communicated quality—and Ball Park already had a notable taste advantage versus competitors in beef hot dogs. All-beef reassured mom, while great taste kept her teens/tweens asking for more.

Having overcome the significant misperceptions among customers, the next challenge was to actually reach out and motivate them to choose Ball Park over the competition. Given that there were, in fact, *two* consumers of the product—teens and their moms, this demand strategy had to follow two distinct tracks.

For moms, having now been convinced of Ball Park's all-beef quality healthfulness, the new message was that the product's ability to satiate hunger *and* its speed of preparation (30 seconds in the microwave to heat, 30 seconds to eat) made it a natural for that crucial afterschool snack for their teen and tween boys. The word quickly spread among both boys and parents—the former liking the simplicity of preparation (as compared to two minutes of microwaving plus a couple more of cooling with most pizzas and snacks like Hot Pockets) and the latter comforted by the safety (no stoves, no burned mouths).

Reaching boys directly was a little more complicated, as their media and communication habits have evolved enormously in just the last decade thanks to the Internet and cell phones. The Ball Park team finally settled on the online gaming sites used by this group, such as Major League Gaming, and circumvented their usual resistance to advertising by creating a Ball Park Top Dog award for gamers to compete for.[25] Ball Park also became among the first nonbeverage brands to promote on skateboarding and BMX biking sites.[26]

While this dual communications strategy cost much less than mass media, it had a significant impact. Within nine months after starting the campaign, we registered an uptick in the number of boys asking for Ball Park by name. Within twelve months, household penetration had grown significantly—3.5 points, faster than any other brand in any category in the Sara Lee family[27]—as moms began buying more Ball Park hot dogs for their boys.

A FINELY TUNED PALATE

The team didn't stop there. Our colleagues at Ball Park now wanted to begin the process of aligning the new market with the product. As yet unanswered was the question of whether the product itself was accurately aligned to these new customers. Teenagers were now asking for, and moms were now willingly purchasing, Ball Park hot dogs. But were the hot dogs they were now eating precisely the ones they wanted?

We were now getting into the very subjective matter of taste. Traditionally, companies deal with these questions in one of two ways:

1. They stick with the product attributes (e.g., taste, texture, sweetness, saltiness, bitterness) that first made them successful, making small modifications over time to gauge market response; or

2. They formulate a new "taste" and then test it via focus groups, panels, tastings, etc., on current and potential customers.

The problem with the first strategy is that it tends to trap the manufacturer in a narrow band of product offerings that offers little opportunity for growth and has a high vulnerability to changes in consumer tastes. The problem with the second strategy is that it is highly dependent on what may prove to be skewed sampling that is not reflective of the real world (think New Coke). Though more expansive in its outlook than the first strategy, it is nevertheless almost always trapped in the existing paradigm (i.e., the supply chain) of the company. That is, it more often reflects "this is what we can deliver" than "this is what we *should* deliver to customers."

There are a large number of tools that a company can use to align a product with market and vice versa. Earlier, you saw the concept of a demand landscape in action, whereby a combination of market research, surveys, and other techniques segments the entire market into an array of individual demand profit pools, each featuring different customer characteristics, tastes, lifestyles, needs, and desires. The sum of all of these demand profit pools is the overall demand landscape.

In constructing just such a demand landscape for Ball Park, we identified six different "motivational" demand profit pools. These six groups represent everything, from food enthusiasts to summer grillers. In doing this, it became apparent to us that Ball Park had built most of its business targeting just one market segment—adult male grillers—that was not even the biggest one.

This narrow targeting became even more obvious when we charted these groups against a second axis, "Life Stage Targets" (households without children, with young children, and with teens). You can see the result in the chart below.

Demand Landscape – Integrating Demand Segments with Life Stages

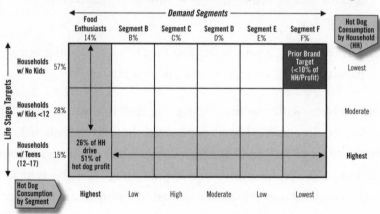

With this demand landscape before us, both Ball Park's market limitations and the sheer magnitude of the opportunity the company (and its competitors) had overlooked are thrown into stark relief.

We had found our untapped market. But we still didn't know if Ball Park's hot dogs matched the "tastes" of that market. So we next turned to another powerful tool for aligning products to their consumers: the "palate map."

The palate map also uses a grid, this time to create a kind of taxonomy of what product characteristics consumers like and don't like, and how they weigh the importance of each of those characteristics.

Here is the palate map for hot dogs. We identified six distinct hot dog palates, defined by the characteristics consumers wanted in an ideal hot dog.

Ideal Hot Dog Palates

	Price Driven			Quality/Taste Driven		
	Value Poultry	**Mild Meat**	**Palate C**	**Palate D**	**Hearty Beef**	**Palate F**
% of HH	A%	B%	C%	D%	E%	F%
Taste/Texture	➢ Firmer bite ➢ Darker color	➢ No extra seasoning ➢ Milder meaty flavor ➢ Softer bite	➢ Features A ➢ Features B ➢ Features C	➢ Features F ➢ Features G ➢ Features H	➢ Great beef flavor ➢ No extra seasoning ➢ Larger, heartier ➢ Firmer bite	➢ Features O ➢ Features P ➢ Features Q ➢ Features R ➢ Features S
Ingredients/ Health	➢ Lower sodium/ fat ➢ Made with poultry	➢ Made with multiple meats	➢ Features D	➢ Features I ➢ Features J ➢ Features K	➢ Made with high quality beef ➢ Not Kosher certified	➢ Features T
Other Characteristics	➢ Best value for the money	➢ More toppings ➢ Great for grilling	➢ Features E	➢ Features L ➢ Features M ➢ Features N	➢ Less toppings, less bun ➢ Great for boiling	➢ Features U ➢ Features V

The six distinct hot dog palates ranged from low-cost poultry up to premium "gourmet" beef hot dogs. We also arrayed these palates against other factors including taste and texture, healthfulness, and other practical characteristics. The result, for the first time anywhere, was a map of what consumers, in all of their diversity, wanted in their hot dogs. In retrospect, this palate map proved to be more influential than any other analytic tool used in this project.

The team discovered another revelation by using the palate map: at the highest end of the market was yet another large and untapped market: "super-premium beef." This niche, which represented not only the most expensive, but also the best-tasting, hot dogs, owned fully 22 percent of the hot dog consumers palate . . . and even more important, it currently represented just 6 percent of the industry's volumes.[28]

There were other revelations as well. For example, this research exploded one of the most common myths about hot dog preparation: it turned out that the better the hot dog, the more likely it was to be *boiled*, not grilled. That's because the high beef content of the premium dogs made them toughen when cooked over a fire. It was the less flavorful meat dogs that got grilled in order to impart more flavor. [Ball Park's chief food scientist, on seeing this news, exclaimed, "If I had known that, I would have developed a different formula!"[29]] The myth about condiments was also backward: the better the hot dog, the *fewer* toppings consumers put on them, wanting to preserve the beef flavor. This had important long-term implications to retail "bundling" of condiments with their hot dog offerings.

Ball Park's sales force also took some lessons from the palate map. Now company salesmen would ask retailers whether they thought consumers in their area were "meat" or "beef" hot dog eaters, and would adjust deliveries accordingly.

What the palate map showed most of all was that there was a disconnect—a significant demand gap—between what the market wanted and what the hot dog industry was delivering. This was underscored by the experience of other comparable industries such as deli meat, beer, and pet food, where the super-premium category inevitably represented about 20 percent of total spending.[30] Better yet, gross margins can be significantly higher in the super-premium market, because taste-oriented consumers (as opposed to price-oriented) will readily accept higher prices for that improved taste. Meanwhile, profit margins increase because the marginal costs don't rise nearly as fast. The result would be a win-win-win: Ball Park would have a lucrative new market, retailers would have a new product offering featuring higher markups, and a large portion of consumers would get the hot dog they'd long been waiting for.

ANALYZING DEMAND

We had now constructed a demand landscape and used it to discover a new and potentially huge untapped demand profit pool: the year-round consumption of hot dogs by teenage boys, purchased by their mothers. Next, we had developed a palate map—and discovered an underdeveloped market (a demand gap) for super-premium hot dogs that, happily, fit neatly with our newly discovered consumers (that is, moms who were concerned about the quality of the food their teens and tweens were eating).

But what did "super-premium" really mean when it came to hot dogs? Was it just the quality of the meat, or flavorings, or were there other factors? For the answer to this, we turned to customer demand analysis. Here's what we found:

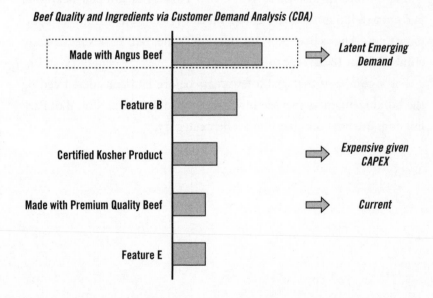

Beef Quality and Ingredients via Customer Demand Analysis (CDA)

Note that when it came to super-premium hot dogs, the critical factor was the quality of the beef, and the most appealing attributes were that the hot dogs were made with Angus beef.

This was good news for Ball Park because, in the case of beef quality, the second and third most popular characteristics (for example, kosher) would be difficult and expensive to achieve. Obtaining Angus beef was mostly a matter of sourcing.[31]

A DEMAND STRATEGY

When it came to understanding demand for Ball Park hot dogs, most of the pieces were now in place. The team had developed a much more precise understanding of demand that identified a new market, new customers, and new products—and together this encompassed a new demand strategy, one that identified a source of highly profitable demand—and designed the approaches to capture it.

In the end, Ball Park hot dogs chose to pursue the new products, markets, and demand profit pools identified by the team.

The result? In just three years, Ball Park sales jumped nearly 40 percent to $400 million (FY 2009), much of that growth from the company's new Angus beef dogs. At the same time, Ball Park's retail share climbed from 18 percent to 21 percent.[32]

For a company that just a few years before had considered ceding the hot dog business to a seemingly unstoppable competitor, Ball Park hot dogs are now number one in their category.[33]

Precisely so.

FIVE

TOTAL INNOVATION

*Finding Unsatisfied Demand
and Fulfilling It*

One of the most extraordinary introductory business meetings The
Cambridge Group ever had took place a few years ago with August
Busch IV, who was then CEO of Anheuser-Busch (A-B), the 150 year-
old beverage giant that leads the beer industry.[1] Busch had called a
week earlier at the suggestion of one of his board members, and asked
to speak with us about a key initiative in A-B's growth strategy.

Anheuser-Busch, as he explained to us, had historically built its
business via the introduction of valuable and innovative new products.[2] However, in the past several years, while the company's existing
lines had prospered, it had been a long time since A-B had enjoyed a
new blockbuster product.

We asked Busch just one question: Does Anheuser-Busch have a
proprietary understanding of unsatisfied demand in its industry, or
does it mostly just invent new beers and then see if there is a market for
that product?

He answered that question by saying, "You're hired."[3]

No one had ever done *that* before. Once we recovered, Busch explained why he had liked our question so much. It seemed that years
before, Anheuser-Busch had brilliantly predicted the rise of the market
for premium water. But because it was also the world's largest buyer of

aluminum cans, the company had decided to put the water into those cans . . . and had missed pioneering the biggest beverage boom in a generation. We only got it half right, Busch told us, because we had given our supply chain precedence over the emerging demand from consumers. If we had been listening, he said, we would have recognized that plastic bottles were the future for bottled water.[4]

Fifteen minutes later we had agreed to work with Anheuser-Busch to help the company identify large pockets of unsatisfied demand that A-B could uniquely fulfill. As we said, it was an extraordinary meeting.

Our first step was to develop an understanding of the demand for beer in America—and then to learn what "need states" were driving the decisions on what beer to drink at different occasions.

We began by conducting what we call a forces and factors analysis to understand the key drivers shaping demand in its three forms: current, latent, and emerging demand. Forces and factors is a macroeconomic analysis that looks outside a specific category in order to find causal factors and trends that are in turn driving change and growth in several business categories around the world. These causal factors ultimately become *hypotheses,* which are then quantitatively tested to determine if one or more of these causal factors can be applied to create growth in the company's own business.

This technique combines secondary research, market research, polls, surveys, and focus group findings to uncover the key elements that are now driving—and shifting—demand.

In Anheuser-Busch's case, the A-B/Cambridge team identified what turned out to be several critical new forces and factors influencing demand. The most important was that by looking at the adjacent alcoholic beverage category, we found that the majority of growth was being shaped by sweeter products, including flavored vodkas.

A-B was already on to this trend, having successfully introduced 9th Street Market and a line extension of the ULTRA brand called ULTRA Fruit. The consistent growth of these sweeter offers led to the hypothesis that a significant percentage of consumers wanted some of their need states, especially the outdoor occasions, to be satisfied by a slightly sweeter-tasting beer.

This went against the industry's long-term view that beer had to be pleasantly bitter. This attribute of beer is measured by brew masters using a scale called International Bitterness Units (IBUs). And the median IBU had suddenly shifted.

The success of these sweeter vodkas, plus Anheuser-Busch's own success with some slightly sweeter beers, led to the hypothesis that there might now be a much larger unsatisfied demand for beer with a sweeter taste than had been previously imagined. If this proved to be true, A-B could preemptively make a major new product introduction, which would have important strategic implications.

- We had the potential for increasing consumption among light-beer drinkers who were consuming sweeter-flavored vodkas;

- We could attract new users to the beer category with a new palate that would align with their unsatisfied demand;

- If the opportunity was as large as some within Anheuser-Busch thought it to be, there was the possibility that pricing power could be achieved.

A MATTER OF TASTE

Even as the team was considering the possibility of an exciting new market based upon a slightly sweeter taste and aimed at a younger, more urban and more ethnic audience, there was a review of the many new products A-B had in development.

Successful innovation is always a combination of an important strategic insight or idea along with the ability to create a great product. Anheuser-Busch was no exception. The innovation team at Anheuser-Busch and their brew masters had created a parade of products featuring every kind of taste and style of beer imaginable. But one stood out.

In fact, it made us sit up in our chairs. We were tasting a light beer with a splash of natural lime. It was different from every other beer on the market, and it had a smooth and delicious taste.

As we were tasting this beer, it became clear the brew had the potential to be the new product that would capture the unsatisfied demand for a sweeter beer. It was not, however, a universally held belief in the beer category that a slightly sweeter beer would be a large marketplace success.

In fact, another major beer brand, Miller, had introduced its own lime-sweetened beer. Unfortunately for Miller, it had gotten the big trend right, but the details wrong. Miller Chill was also a lime-flavored beer, but beyond that, all similarities with the proposed Anheuser-Busch product ended. Miller Chill used artificial lime flavoring and added salt to the product. A-B was looking for something different, and it was guided by a "Palate Map," which clarified the specific taste attributes and benefits consumers were seeking.

A-B conducted some pub taste tests and knew they were on the right path. Miller's product was off the mark. The salt reduced the sweetness consumers experienced when adding a slice of lime to Corona. And the artificial lime flavoring resulted in a noticeable after-taste. The net result was that Miller Chill had a slightly tart taste that was not at all what consumers were hoping for.

While having hypotheses about unsatisfied demand is critical to successful innovation, the commitment of significant resources can and should only come when there is compelling quantitative and economic data that confirms the hypotheses.

The A-B/Cambridge team did a rigorous piece of research in order to validate the specific consumers who seemed to have an unsatisfied demand for a sweeter beer. This was the work that would confirm or deny the critical strategic objectives: Would the new product increase beer consumption among light-beer drinkers, would the new product attract new users to the beer category, and could pricing power be established?

Within a few short weeks, the answers came back and they were everything A-B had hoped for and more. The team now had a quantitative and economic fact base that showed there were, indeed, high levels of unsatisfied demand for exactly the product the A-B innovation team and the brew masters had in mind.

A multiphase effort began to unfold. The brew masters created twenty-six different product samples. They were then tested with the specific consumer targets whose unsatisfied demand the team wanted to satisfy.

While many of the products passed every taste hurdle, one emerged as virtually the perfect new-tasting beer that A-B had been searching for. A separate team designed a fresh package that turned out to fully capture both the new beer palate as well as its intended outdoor usage occasion. Yet another team worked with A-B's internal leaders as well as with a large group of beer wholesalers in order to talk about the new concept but also to conduct taste tests with beer wholesalers.

Everything came together. The enthusiasm was growing for a new and potentially very important market innovation.

Included in these conversations with Anheuser-Busch's internal and external leadership groups was the question of whether or not this new sweetened beer could be branded as part of the Bud Light family. This was no small question: Bud Light is the world's largest-selling beer—and you step lightly before making even the smallest changes in a product that is so successful.

In truth, there was a lot of initial resistance to the idea. In a category that was largely consumed by men, would a sweeter beer cause erosion in the parent brand? Or would it broaden the perception of Bud Light and attract new users to the brand—all while fulfilling the demand for an emerging need state based around outdoor beer (rather than sports) occasions?

A decision of this magnitude required rigorous testing beforehand, and the team now had the very positive results. Led by Dave Peacock, currently the CEO of Anheuser-Busch, every possible avenue had been explored in order to guarantee a risk-free decision.

"Even the loudest naysayers were convinced once the data came back," says Peacock. "Not only would Bud Light Lime add incremental volume, it would broaden and strengthen the perception of Bud Light. So, while filling a gap in our portfolio, we would also be adding an important dimension to Bud Light of being appropriate for outdoor active occasions in addition to our long and successful brand perception of being young and social."

And that was only the beginning. "As a company, we experienced what it's like to find unsatisfied demand and fulfill it in more ways than one," Peacock continues. "Not only did Bud Light Lime create a unique product for a new pool of demand—as well as broaden the perception of the brand—it also proved to be a bigger financial success than we ever imagined. When the two segments of consumers who were the primary targets were asked how much they would be willing to pay for the product, they told us they'd pay more for Bud Light Lime than for Bud Light because it was so innovative. The power of finding unsatisfied demand and fulfilling it also showed us that if a level of demand is high enough, you can also gain pricing power at the same time," concludes Peacock.

Bud Light Lime was formally introduced to the public on May 5 (Cinco de Mayo), 2008. From the very beginning, Bud Light Lime was an enormous success. It sold four times the amount of Miller Chill that had been sold in the past year, and in just half the time. Sales were also double that of Blue Moon, the previous year's beer phenomenon.

Meanwhile, the cannibalization by Bud Light Lime on traditional Bud Light sales was even lower than had been predicted. Profits and margins increased due to pricing power, and the objective of bringing in light-beer drinkers and increasing their consumption was fully realized. In addition, approximately 8 percent of Bud Light Lime drinkers turned out to be nonbeer drinkers—meaning that the company was bringing back some of the consumers who had until recently migrated away from beer to flavored vodkas.

In the months that followed, data showed that following Bud Light Lime's introduction, the entire Bud Light brand enjoyed an uptick in perceived "coolness" and trendiness.

Anheuser-Busch now had its most successful new product in years, and the company was now beautifully positioned to move into new and evolving markets—all from a product that had been shelved just months before.

Bud Light Lime was ultimately ranked the number-one new product launch in the consumer goods industry during 2008.

MYTH-FREE INNOVATION

Of all of the activities that companies engage in, *innovation* may be the one that is most mythologized, misperceived, and misunderstood. According to studies, American corporations spend more than $1 trillion per year on innovation,[5] and only get a fraction of that back in return on their investment, in large part because of this misperception.

This confusion begins right at the start, with the very definition of the word. In everyday usage, "innovation" is perceived as a creative exercise. It is nothing of the sort; in truth, at least in the world of business, *innovation is a disciplined, demand-based process.*

If that statement is surprising, it is probably because the term is so often attached to the image of a scientist or engineer in a lab somewhere having a "Eureka!" moment. But that isn't innovation, that's *invention*—which is a very different thing. Innovation often incorporates invention, but it also encompasses much more, and ultimately, innovation must be tested in the marketplace.

We would go so far as to make the statement that there has never been a successful long-term innovation that did not better satisfy an existing or emerging customer demand.

That suggests a definition:

Innovation is finding unsatisfied profitable demand and then fulfilling it.

Understanding this new definition is the key to consistent, successful innovation. Sure, creativity plays a part—it will likely be the source, if you are lucky enough to have it happen, of that one-in-a-million invention that transforms both your company and your industry. But in the end, even that brainstorm will have to meet the standard of satisfying unfulfilled demand.

Edison famously spoke of invention being a little bit of inspiration and a lot of perspiration.[6] Innovation is the same thing, with much of that sweat being expended on understanding what the market wants.

TOTAL INNOVATION

You'll note that in defining innovation, we placed no constraints on where that innovation may occur. That was intentional, because a big mistake companies make is to narrow their idea of what innovation should result in, typically focusing on new products alone.

It is also worth noting that the word "innovation" itself has a way of freezing people in their tracks. Over and over we've heard people say, "I'm just not a creative person, so I can't be very good at innovation." That's why, when Jim Kilts was CEO of Gillette; he and his SVP of strategy, Peter Klein, took the pressure off of everyone at Gillette by reframing the entire topic. They told the company to stop referring to innovation and to just "find a better way."[7]

Kilts and Klein then applied what they called the "Total Innovation" process at Gillette to great effect.[8] While Gillette had enjoyed a reputation as a highly innovative company, the truth was that its innovation pipeline and innovation successes were running out of steam in the years before Kilts and Klein arrived. Within six months of putting the Total Innovation process in place, Gillette's revenues increased by approximately 15 percent and net income jumped by more than 18 percent.[9] While there were arguably other factors at play contributing to Gillette's financial success during this time, for example favorable exchange rates and a series of hurricanes spurring battery sales, the Total Innovation process was clearly a major contributing factor to Gillette's success. With the new innovation process and a new confidence throughout the organization—all begun by taking the pressure off the need to be "creative"—Gillette began to post double-digit revenue gains each year after having suffered several years of declining revenues.

As we learned by working with Kilts and Klein at Gillette, real innovation is *total innovation*. That is, it begins, like all new products or services, with the idea or market analysis—but it continues all of the way through the manufacturing process, packaging, distribution, retail, consumption, and even beyond, through that product's or service's entire lifespan. In a world of oversupply and flattening demand, this is the only strategy that assures that all of the potential profit is realized from the process, and that the product or service itself is precisely aligned with the most important demand pools. The number of ways that total innovation can be applied to a particular product or service may surprise you. Here are some examples:

• *Invention* The development of breakthrough technical solutions that provide new-to-the-world customer benefits, can range from the mythic "category makers" such as the World Wide Web and the Apple Macintosh, to fine-tuned solutions such as the thin-walled plastic water bottle and frozen yogurt pops.

• *New Product Innovation* The application of existing technologies to deliver benefits in a new and compelling way, are new-to-the-company innovations. The Swiffer floor sweeper and iPod MP3 player are classic examples.

• *Product Enhancement Innovation* These are new-to-the-product innovations, and typically involve varying an existing feature or adding a new one to enhance the product's perceived benefits. The iPod Touch, new flavors of Gatorade, and Chocolate Crème-Filled Oreos are examples.

• *Commercial (Nonproduct) Innovation* These are new-to-the-channel innovations that take existing products and find new ways to deliver greater value to customers through innovative channel, packaging, and merchandising solutions. Examples include the Duracell Power Station in-store display, and Coca-Cola's Fridge Pack soda can holder.

• *Operational Innovation* As you might guess, these are new-to-the-company operations innovations—process or service enhancements that may or may not directly impact the customer, but ultimately improve overall competitive position. Wal-Mart's cross-docking supply chain logistics, Progressive's claims processing approach, and most famous of all, Ray Kroc's pioneering work rethinking the nature of fast food preparation are examples.

• *Business Model Innovation* These are new-to-the-organization innovations—that is, redesigning the process of how a product or service is produced, delivered, or used, to provide greater value to the end user. Many of these innovations are legendary: direct store delivery, the Sears catalog, the Ford Model T assembly line, the Sloan/General Motors divisional model, and Hewlett-Packard's management by objective.

As you can see, if you think of innovation as merely new product development or packaging, you may be missing both crucial sources of new revenues and profits, as well as powerful competitive advantages. But staying innovative across the organization, not just in the R&D lab, is difficult and requires constant vigilance. It certainly requires senior managers to make innovation a clear priority throughout the organization without attempting to micromanage the process along the way. Ultimately, it comes down to leading by example: the way a

CEO and senior management lead, define, and consistently encourage and apply innovation in an organization sets the pattern for everyone else. It is the difference between sustained, predictable real growth and mere lip service. Innovation is not a one-time thing; it is a culture. It isn't a destination, but a process.

THE VALUE OF INNOVATION

Given our definition of successful innovation—*finding unsatisfied profitable demand and fulfilling it*—one can intuit that managing innovation, while depending on some measure of creativity, is truly a process in which you can almost always be sure of success.

And success breeds success. As we'll now show, a reputation for being an innovator has its own rewards. Wall Street puts a premium on predictable profit growth, and one of the best indicators of that growth in the future is a company's track record of successful innovation in the present. This is why there is so much focus on innovation, and why it is the subject of cover stories for *Fortune*, *BusinessWeek*, and other business publications.

When innovation works, it is extremely profitable. Innovation can increase sales, grow margins, motivate the sales organization, increase asset utilization, redefine your market and your competition, and ultimately even reinvent your company, your market, and sometimes society itself.

As authors Clayton Christensen and Michael Raynor noted in *The Innovator's Solution*,[10] the expected returns from new investment in innovation can account for well over half of a firm's total market value. For companies such as Dell, Johnson & Johnson, Procter & Gamble, and General Electric, expected returns from innovation can drive more than 60 percent—and sometimes as much as 80 percent—of market value. The top 20 percent of companies that successfully drive innovation deliver four times the total shareholder returns that the bottom 20 percent do.

But the key word here is "successful." A lot of companies try to be successful innovators, and spend as much as 10 percent of their profits every year in pursuit of that reputation, but few ever make it—usually because they deviate from our definition in pursuit of the ever elusive "game changer."

As the new demand economy continues to assert itself, we can expect this correlation between innovation and market value to grow even stronger, even as companies are forced to cut back on their R&D budgets. This in turn suggests an economy of the future with fewer successful innovators that enjoy ever bigger financial rewards.

One reason for this is that in an economy dominated by demand; the connections between the tangible assets of supply (such as inventory) have an increasingly tenuous connection to a firm's overall market value. The numbers are stunning: in 1978, 95 percent of the market value for 3,500 assessed companies was explained by book value. By 1998, that same book value explained only 28 percent of market value.[11] Intangible assets, not least the ability of a company to stay competitive with new products and services, now dominate the perceived value of modern enterprises.

In the last two decades, economists have begun to describe this "capability" side of intangible assets as "intellectual" or knowledge capital, and they have begun to measure such once-obscure metrics as patent filings, number of PhDs on staff, academic citations, and so on to attach some empirical values to a company's ability to regularly come up with new products and services.

And their research has borne fruit. For example, it has been shown that the correlation between stock returns and intellectual capital is much higher (at .53) than the correlation with earnings (.29).[12] Other research suggests that every new patent citation gained by a company increases its market value by about 3 percent.[13] Given those kinds of financial prizes, it's no wonder that billions of dollars each year are poured into innovation operations in companies around the world, from the giant R&D operations of Fortune 50 corporations to tiny skunkworks in garage start-ups.

Beyond the significant upside from innovation is the stark reality that perhaps the biggest benefit of being an "innovation company" is that continual, successful innovation will be critical to survival in a rapidly changing, technology-driven world with dramatically shorter product life cycles. Unless your innovation is patent protected (and assuming those patents are honored across global markets), competitors will reverse-engineer and replicate your offers with incredible speed. You can be certain your competitor is looking for the next "killer app." And you need to beat them to it with an innovative new product or service that you already know will succeed.

ALIGNING INNOVATION

As we all know, many innovation efforts fall well short and do not deliver the desired revenue and profit growth that companies seek. While there is no innovation approach that can guarantee success, we would be remiss if we did not at least revisit the range of reasons so many of these innovation efforts fall short—and suggest why one technique almost always works.

One big mistake companies often make in the innovation arena is to narrow their idea of what innovation should result in, typically focusing on new products alone. In doing so, they often close the door on more (and often bigger) opportunities for innovation than those that remain. This negligence usually isn't enough to make the new product a failure, but it has left a lot of companies stuck with stellar but underpriced or undermarketed products that never achieve their full potential profitability. All of that time and money was invested to pioneer a new market with a great new product—and with next to nothing to show for it.

A similarly critical mistake in traditional consumer innovation is the practice of assigning to a small group of people within marketing the responsibility of convincing the rest of the organization that the innovation they have is in fact a successful and highly profitable innovation. In fact, innovation is only consistently successful if representatives from every critical function participate from the very start—so that they perform a reality check at the beginning before the company wastes time and resources. That way, they can head off something that can never be profitable, that doesn't align with the company's core competencies. Having all critical functions on board throughout the process, you can greatly increase the probability for success.

The fundamental reality is that all too often in business, good ideas formulated by the people "responsible" for innovation (such as the corporate labs) are not shared with the people who will be responsible for making, sourcing, distributing, selling, and maintaining the product—but instead are thrown over the wall to them as a fait accompli they are expected to sell somehow.

In the next sections, we will discuss the critical elements of the successful total innovation process and means to ensure these common pitfalls are a thing of the past.

IDENTIFY AND REALIZE

As we've said, innovation is also a process. And a successful innovation process is typically divided into two parts: identification and realization.

The identification process is itself a series of steps. Let's look at each of them more closely.

• *Investigation* Especially now, in the new demand-driven global economy, you must begin the innovation process by finding pools of untouched demand and formulating a hypothesis for how to satisfy that demand. Then, most important of all, you build a quantified business case that, if you satisfy this demand, it will be profitable.

• *Prioritization* Most companies have more good ideas than they have resources to implement. And if you adopt the principles of total innovation, those good ideas may come from every corner of your company and address every one of your operations. That's why you need to continually prioritize these opportunities based on how much they will contribute to the bottom line.

• *Inspiration* The previous steps focused on improving what you've already got. But that still leaves some big holes, particularly in new strategic growth opportunities for which there may be no precedent and little information. Those are opportunities for some real creative thinking, and you should use all of the tricks that creative people bring to these kinds of problems—brainstorming, analogy, mash-ups of other successful ideas, intuition, and so on. Needless to say, these inspired ideas—no matter how brilliant they may seem—still must be put through and survive the investigation process.

• *Optimization* You've now identified your best ideas, tested them in the crucible of market analysis, and prioritized them. The next step is to take the winners and present them in a controlled setting (such as a focus group) to your target demand profit pools and/or your "super consumers"—that is, the people who are most likely to be the heaviest users or needers of your potential innovation ideas—and see what they think. Their input is crucial because they typically care the most, know the most, and set the highest standards for your product. If you can satisfy these users, you can be certain that you can satisfy the more casual user. (It was at just such a session that we ran a number of years ago for Sears about credit cards where just such a super consumer said, simply, "All I really care about is the minimum payment" . . . and thus the low minimum payment strategy was introduced to the credit card industry.[14])

• *Validation* In this final step of the identification process, you bring to bear a number of traditional analytic tools—quantitative determination of acceptance levels, estimated sales volume, aggregate demand, sourcing—to help you make a business case for that innovation. What began as a largely subjective process now takes on the shape of formal logic: *If* we do this, *then* we will create this much business, grow this much, and make this much profit.

SATISFYING DEMAND

If you look at every innovation success, from the wheel to today's latest hot electronic device, you will see without exception a product or idea that improved on what already existed. Every single one has met the demands of our definition of innovation.

It should also be no surprise that innovations that have failed—the Ford Edsel, Clear Pepsi, New Coke, smokeless cigarettes, Duncan Hines Soft Batch Cookies—usually did so because they did *not* better satisfy customers' demand.

But how do you know, especially with a really innovative product or service, if the demand is actually there? How can you guarantee that you've fulfilled that part of our definition? Well, we already showed you one aspect of the total innovation process that has you cast your net wider to increase the likelihood of finding good, clearly defined markets. The next step (as we're about to see) is the realization process, which, by bringing in all of the players in the process for a reality check, can often identify which apparent pools of demand are in fact mirages.

At the very beginning of identification, admittedly the fuzzy front end of innovation, each proposition must start the investigation with a hypothesis about where in one's business there is unfulfilled demand, either in a particular product or across a category. The hypotheses are, in fact, developed by analyzing the market from a number of perspectives, the most important of these being the forces and factors analysis we described earlier.

In practice, forces and factors analysis examines the causal market forces and industry factors that shape and drive current, latent, and emerging demand. To conduct this analysis, several approaches need to be leveraged to help uncover new insights into the drivers of demand.

Market Macro Trends   These can include demographic shifts, societal trends, economic conditions, and technological changes that are shaping the market. Another powerful source of new innovation hypotheses is analogous product or service categories. What might the kids' skateboard market tell you about kids' shoes? Or the latest popular bar drinks about changing tastes in desserts?

Global Precedents   External forces and factors should include analyses of other regions of the world. What can businesses in the United States facing the upcoming retirement of the baby boomers learn from the ways Japan has coped with its burgeoning senior population? Famously, it was the neighborhood coffee houses of Italy that inspired Starbucks's founder, Howard Schultz, to start the ubiquitous coffee chain.[15]

The Market Landscape   This analysis includes an understanding of target consumers, competitors, manufacturing systems, distribution channels, and technology, to uncover further hypotheses on how internal and external capabilities and competences can be leveraged to serve some unfulfilled demand. This process also must reach beyond the R&D lab to embrace every operation in the company, including the folks who understand customers, pricing, the supply chain, the impact on company culture, resources, patents and copyrights, and most of all, the employees with the power to say "no."

"I BELIEVE THAT . . ."

Forces and factors analysis should ultimately produce important insights into current consumer segments, behaviors, desires, and need gaps. It should also identify new demand that has just emerged, is about to emerge, and will likely emerge in the future. Finally, it should offer some intriguing clues as to how other industries in other markets and in other parts of the world have come up with clever solutions that you can imitate, modify, or license.

From these data, you should be able to either prove the existence of the untapped demand you've already hypothesized, or uncover some new opportunities—and construct hypotheses for them.

The next step of this process is to bring all of these hypotheses together by defining a set of "strategic growth opportunity areas" (SGOAs). Each SGOA should be characterized by starting with the words "I believe that . . ." and finishing the sentence with a clear statement of the nature of the unmet demand and your company's ability to provide a potential solution. This step allows you to narrow down your attention to a workable space instead of facing that yawning chasm produced by the question, "Where will I find the Next Big Thing?"

Now, instead, you are working with a defined set of possible places where there really is a problem to be solved, where a meaningful improvement can make a difference, and where you need to dig deeper in order to find the right solution. Essentially, the "I believe that . . . " step represents an early hypothetical business case for each SGOA. If it is hard or impossible to make this such a clear and simple statement for the idea, it is not yet a potential innovation.

Once these SGOAs are determined, they need to be assessed according to their relative potential and whittled down to a manageable number of opportunities by selecting only those with the greatest promise and strategic value.

The next step (which we call "safari" because it is often an extended search in unfamiliar country) is the process of optimizing the concepts surrounding each of these SGOAs in conversation with consumers in the targeted demand profit pools. This approach, which is similar to a gap analysis, compares the benefit of the proposed product or service to the current offerings in the market. The process both sharpens the definition of the idea and offers yet another opportunity to sort out those innovations with the greatest potential.

Finally, the remaining SGOAs are subjected to a "quantitative consumer assessment" that answers the question: If I take this to market what will be the outcome? What market share will we win? Among which consumers? Who will we win that share from . . . our own portfolio or from competitors? What are the economics? The right answers enable the innovation to continue down the pathway to realization.

Here, graphically, is what the whole customer identification process looks like.

Total Innovation Process—Identification

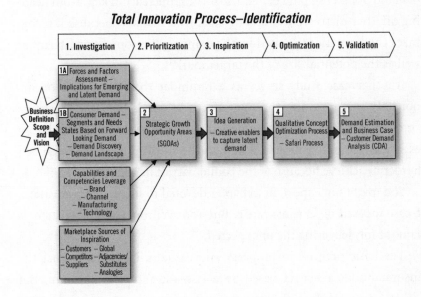

IN GOOD HANDS

The second half of the innovation process is "realization." This is the process of actually bringing the product to market—for which, unlike the identification first half, there is an abundance of tools and processes, as well as methodologies taught in every business school. The realization process is structured along the lines of the widely used Stage-Gate process which systematically assesses ideas by using technical, manufacturing, distribution, selling, and financial hurdles, among other evaluations.

The lesson to be learned from the example of companies such as

Apple and Gillette is that some companies have developed a robust, repeatable process for innovation success, and they consistently reap rewards for having integrated that process into their operations. Meanwhile, other companies spend fortunes in support of innovation, yet come away with little to show for it.

Successful innovation is *focused*, *disciplined*, *realistic* innovation. Focused, because it knows its target: an untapped but highly profitable demand pool. Disciplined, because it is channeled and kept from heading off after distractions and tangents. And realistic, because it recognizes the limitations created by the company's resources and talent as well as the potential size of the target market.

Another case study serves as a reminder that innovation occurs not only in companies that manufacturer goods but also in service companies—even venerable ones. In addition, this case provides an example of the invention of a new-to-the-world product that is much harder to achieve because of the complexity of its industry.

You might not expect, in a chapter devoted to successful innovation, a case focused on car insurance. But Tom Wilson, CEO of Allstate, is famous for delivering the unexpected.

The basic premise in property and casualty insurance is that the insurer builds a matrix based on a risk-and-return continuum. But Allstate sees it differently. "What we try to do is consumer or demand driven," says Wilson. "We look at the products we offer and the service we deliver on the basis of what the consumer wants and how he or she thinks about our business."[16]

Contrary to the popular view, auto insurance has had its share of innovations. It's just that they've mostly been on the pricing side. In Illinois alone, for example, there are more than 1 billion different possible prices for car insurance based on a very sophisticated pricing algorithm.[17]

As one of the true leaders in pricing, in 2004, Allstate knew that it had a competitive advantage. In fact, so supremely confident was the firm that company management believed that if Allstate lost a client on price, it was probably a good thing—because the folks at Allstate had correctly assessed the risk/reward ratio, and some other competitor out there had made a mistaken calculation.

But now Tom Wilson set out to shake things up. Where most of Allstate's competitors focused on this price risk vector, Wilson asked his people to understand the market in a different way. "What if we really understood the differences in customer types and the benefits they wanted from insurance?" Wilson asked his leadership team. "Then we could apply our advantage in competitive pricing based on the different demand that consumers have for automobile insurance. In other words, let's see if we can differentiate and win by understanding more about customer demand than our competitors do."[18]

The first step was to create an understanding of the demand for auto insurance, and how it varied among different types of consumers. At the time Allstate began its work, Geico was becoming a much more formidable competitor. Its online business model, which appealed to an increasing number of consumers with the simple message of "We'll save you 15 percent," was gaining traction in the marketplace. In almost any industry, when a competitor begins to grow rapidly, most companies get diverted and try to match that competitor in order to share in its success. And that would certainly have been the easy thing for Allstate to do.

Instead, Allstate's desire to understand consumer demand turned out to offer a view of the market that was not only clear but revelatory.

In fact, about 40 percent of the market did want lower prices.[19] And many of Allstate's competitors were only too happy to compete on the basis of price. But what the data also showed Allstate was that there was another 40 percent who wanted more benefits.

The existence of that other large cohort seeking more benefits was very good news to Allstate. Its more than 12,000 agents[20] were in the business of delivering a high level of personalized service, and thus were in a perfect position to communicate the new benefits Allstate would pursue, one customer at a time.

It's rare to find an innovation directed at an entire market. It is much more frequently the case that a company identifies a group of segments or a group of demand profit pools that it can serve best and most profitability. It's the ability to align your business model with the consumers who have unsatisfied demand that is critical to having successful and profitable innovation.

Now that Allstate knew that a large chunk of consumers wanted more benefits, the company set about exploring precisely which types of benefits these consumers wanted most. And what it found these customers wanted most was what they called "fairness," but that Allstate quickly realized was *reciprocity.*

What customers told Allstate was that when they bought insurance, they wanted to put their complete trust in that auto insurance company to protect them if they had an accident. But, they continued, they never knew whether this would be the case until after they had an accident and filed a claim. These consumers saw this as one-sided, with all the leverage on the side of the insurance company.

The Allstate team, led by Ed Biemer, saw it differently. What if you could take this uncertainty out of the relationship, asked Biemer, and replace it with reciprocity and certainty?[21] And thus was born a series of new features such as expanded Accident Forgiveness and a Safe Driver Bonus—not terms one was likely to hear in an auto insurance company, at least not until Allstate began to build their understanding of consumer demand.

You've undoubtedly seen the Allstate spokesman, Dennis Haysbert, talk about the company's proprietary Your Choice Auto, the program in which Allstate guarantees not to raise your premium in the event you have an accident.

Consumers were elated. For the first time, an insurance company was willing to guarantee them that under virtually all circumstances, Allstate would guarantee *not* to raise their premium just because of an accident. For those drivers who did not have an accident, there was something new as well: they could receive a Safe Driver Bonus of about 5 percent of their premium. The impact was immediate—but more about that later.

Notice that the branding for this new offer was called "Your Choice Auto." That's because not only did consumers want reciprocity and certainty, they also wanted choice. Some wanted a Platinum version of Your Choice Auto, some wanted a less expensive Gold product, and still others wanted a Value product. The big breakthrough was that consumers now knew they got to make the choice. It changed the way they perceived how auto insurance worked and it enabled them to define the economic relationship they wanted with Allstate.

Once Allstate talked with some of the consumers who wanted more benefits, it found that Accident Forgiveness was a true magnet. We can go still further, Wilson and Biemer announced to the company. If Accident Forgiveness is the magnet that attracts consumers, what's the glue that will keep them with Allstate?

The answer came, as you would expect, from the consumers who had that unsatisfied demand. It would be great, they said, if we were rewarded for each year that we were accident-free by having our deductibles reduced. So, for example, if we had a $500 deductible and were accident free for three years, our deductible would become only $200.

Okay, said Wilson, we'll offer Accident Forgiveness, a Safe Driving Bonus, and a declining deductible because it will differentiate us from our competitors. At the same time it will enable us to align with and satisfy the demand of the auto insurance customer who wants more benefits.[22]

To deliver on the promise of Your Choice Auto, the Allstate team incorporated the new learnings about consumer demand into the launch for the new offer and into the way it does business. As a result, Allstate's brand positioning, marketing communications, sales training, and follow-up customer contacts were all aligned with Your Choice Auto and the underlying consumer demand it reflects. Meanwhile, to protect its innovation from being copied by competitors, Allstate filed patent applications, another unusual move in the insurance industry.

Was it worthwhile for Allstate to look at its customers through a different lens? Was it time well spent to identify unsatisfied demand? According to Wilson, approximately $4 billion in Your Choice products are sold each year.[23] Not only that, but they are sold at a higher average revenue per policy and the customers stay longer. And that of course translates to a higher lifetime value. So is successful innovation possible in every business? The Allstate case argues the answer is: Absolutely. All you have to do is identify the unsatisfied demand and fulfill it. But first you have to have leadership that wants to explore the boundaries and gives the company the freedom to go where the consumer takes them.

In 2006, Allstate's senior management team agreed to a new vision. They called it the "Shared Vision with the customer in the center," and it plans to reinvent Allstate as a fully customer-demand-driven enterprise.

"We're going to reinvent our company for the customer," says Wilson. "We want the customer to know that we've got their back."[24]

THE VALUE OF FAILURE

It was marketing guru Regis McKenna who famously said that Silicon Valley, generally regarded as the most innovative business community on earth, is most defined by failure"[25] By this, he meant that it takes a large number of failed products, services, companies, and initiatives to create that handful of successful innovations that drive the technology revolution forward. And because of that, Silicon Valley has developed a culture that, if it doesn't reward failure, certainly respects honorable failures and tries to learn from them.

As the history of Silicon Valley has shown, this appetite for risk despite the potential for failure is a powerful process for the creation of radical new products and fast-moving new industries. But it is a brutal process, too, with a high mortality rate among young companies.

For individual companies, this is a hard way to live—and die. What established companies want is strong, continuous growth and healthy, defensible markets. And yet, too often, they pursue the Silicon Valley model of innovation: perpetually chasing that new "home run" product, the game changer that will secure the company's fortunes forever.

It doesn't work. Perpetual breakthrough innovation is all but impossible, even in companies built specifically around that strategy (as we'll see later in the story of Motorola). If you want to build a company that wins *and lasts*, you need a strategy that combines continual innovation that is both targeted toward, and refined by, the people who will use that innovation. That means enlisting those customers in product design via crowdsourcing and other forms of community-based design, user groups, shared code and open systems, and previewing products while still in their alpha and beta stages. It also means providing them with entrepreneurial opportunities—such as the Apple iStore—that enable them to bring their own intellectual capital to bear on improving the total experience of your product or service. And it means soliciting the help of this army of supporters for everything from sales and marketing, to early warning about competitive threats, to aftermarket products, service, and support.

It was precisely because of their high mortality rate that Silicon Valley companies recognized first these new roles for their customers. Customer participation has proven to be the crucial competitive advantage for Apple and Google, among others—and it is the very basis for the existence of companies like Twitter, Craigslist, eBay, Wikipedia, and YouTube.

Not only does customer participation in the innovation process massively force-multiply the brainpower brought to the task (for free!) but, because these consumers are in effect designing for themselves, what they produce is almost always perfectly targeted. And isn't this exactly what you are looking for in your own innovation strategy?

SIX

THE PRICE IS RIGHT

Finding the Right Price (At Last)

It is a truth universally acknowledged in the business world that *nobody ever thinks their pricing is right.*

It is also a truth that they are usually correct.

Pricing strategy is often the one area where managers feel least confident about their approach. On the one hand, these managers recognize that if they price their offerings too low, they risk leaving money on the table. And on the other hand, if they set prices too high they risk losing valuable consumers or customers; or just as bad, risk pricing themselves out of the retail or distribution channels they need to reach those customers. It is a dichotomy that haunts almost every business on the planet: lose profits or lose customers.

Surely there is a better way, one that ends not with compromise, but a win.

In fact, there is. And once again, it begins with taking a closer look at demand. We'll start this investigation of pricing by presenting five basic principles:

- There are no commodity markets, just commodity marketing approaches.

- The foundation of any successful pricing strategy is to price to demand, not to markets.

- The value equation for target consumers is optimized by understanding the ratio of benefits delivered for the price charged.

- Driving meaningful differentiation in your products is what separates you from competitors and what commands pricing premiums.

- Success with these first four principles creates the opportunity to be a market maker that sets prices or commands price premiums, rather than a price taker that merely accepts commodity prices.

We'll revisit these principles in a moment. What's important to understand now is that there really is a rational and systematic way to price products and services in such a way as to escape the lost profits/ lost customers dichotomy. Better yet, this kind of intelligent, demand-driven pricing can actually uncover *new* sources of customers and profits. And that can be a very valuable advantage.

How valuable? The numbers are so compelling and decisive that it is astonishing to us that every future manager isn't taught this in business school. A 1 percent price increase has a *50 percent* greater impact on operating income than does a 1 percent decrease in variable cost.[1] More remarkably, that same 1 percent price increase has a *215 percent* greater impact on operating profit than a 1 percent volume increase in sales.[2]

Why don't most managers know this? It's like the old cartoon of the store owner who, on being told that he was losing money on every unit sold, announces, "Don't worry, we'll make it up in volume." If you can find a way to raise the price of your product or service by just a few percent—through more targeted marketing, by improving product image, by finding more lucrative profit pools, or by adding new features without adding cost—the impact on your bottom line will be so great that almost no realistic amount of cost cutting or increased production will be able to match it.

PRICING POWER

Then why is so much attention paid to cutting overhead and increasing production and so little to intelligent pricing strategies?

We don't think it's a lack of desire. After all, what company would turn down the opportunity to earn some attractive pricing premiums—especially if they require little added cost or effort. What's stopping them? We think there are two interrelated obstacles. The first, frankly, is that developing a pricing strategy can become a fairly complex process, given all of the inputs used and decisions to be made. These can include your own portfolio of products, competitive products and how they are priced, the margins required by channel partners, promotions, discounts, and the realities of fast-moving markets, to just name a few. Without some clear principles to guide the approach to pricing strategy, it can quickly become overwhelming. The second is that there is a general lack of a fundamental framework to develop an optimized pricing strategy that incorporates the five principles we listed above.

It is also getting harder for most companies to compete on pricing. For two decades now, pricing power has eroded across the economy. It is yet another indicator of the transition from a supply-driven economy to a demand-driven economy[3] that, comparing the interval from 1991 to the present, with the period from the 1947 to 1990, business-to-business (B2B) pricing power has eroded nearly 80 percent, while business-to-consumer (B2C) pricing power has eroded by 35 percent. This means, on the one hand, that finding opportunities to leverage smart pricing strategy is tougher than ever; but on the other hand, that executing such a strategy is also perhaps more important than ever before.

This loss of pricing power also means that businesses can no longer rely on the simple pricing formulas—such as "cost-plus" pricing—

at served them well enough in the past. Under cost-plus pricing, businesses set their prices by calculating the total cost of making and distributing their products or services and then adding to it the profit margin they were seeking. As a technique, it wasn't fancy (and it often left a lot of money on the table), but it worked well enough in a marketplace where demand generally matched or exceeded supply.

The downside was that cost-plus pricing freed companies from ever having to develop their pricing "muscles." They never had to become skillful at managing pricing, or to develop a pricing framework. Instead, most companies relied on cutting costs, improving productivity, and achieving scale—ironically, much more difficult challenges than that of simply being smart about prices.

They can't ignore pricing anymore, not least because that astounding impact of a 1 percent price increase on the bottom line works in the other direction as well: the ongoing erosion of pricing power. In this new environment, pricing is no longer an afterthought, it is now a key competitive factor.

Why? Because even in the current environment of eroding pricing power, as well as flattening—or even contracting—demand, businesses can develop a more precise profit-building approach by following those five basic principles of a demand-driven pricing strategy we just enumerated. Let's list them again, in a more concise form, and then look at them in depth.

1. Price to demand profit pools, not to markets.

2. Leverage the value equation: Value = Benefits/Price

3. Drive differentiation that is critical to pricing power.

4. Build and manage a logical "good, better, best" price trade-up architecture.

5. Be a market maker, not a price taker.

FINDING TRUE VALUE

Principle #1: Pricing to demand profit pools within markets, rather than to entire markets, is critical for long-term success.

Experience has taught us that whenever products and services are priced to broad markets, businesses inevitably leave money on the table. This is because aggregating to the mean—that is, pricing to the average—always means forgoing the potential to earn a higher profit margin from those specific demand profit pools willing to pay a price premium for benefits currently being "given away." In effect, the differentiating benefits you worked so hard to add to your offers are now free.

By comparison, while pricing to those high-profit pools may mean losing some price-conscious customers (who are typically low-profit promotional buyers anyway), that loss—remember our 1 percent number—is more than recouped by pricing at a premium to the high-profit demand.

Here's an example from everyday life: consider how most movie theaters charge for tickets. With the exception of a few discounts for children, seniors, and some matinee show times, almost every moviegoer pays the same price to see a given film.[4] Thus those who arrive early enough to a crowded screening get the best seats at the fixed price. Meanwhile, that same price is paid by folks who are running late, even though they may have to make some major compromises such as not sitting together or sitting uncomfortably close to the screen.

This is the way it has always been. Yet a very different pricing model is used for similar forms of entertainment such as live drama, sporting events, and concerts. These venues charge a premium for the best seats, as well as reserve-seat locations in advance.

By comparison, thanks to the Web today's American moviegoer (in parts of Europe you can reserve seats) who is too busy to arrive early at least has the option of guaranteeing a seat in the theater through such services as Fandango, which allow them to go online and, by paying a premium for reserve tickets. Clearly, the success of Fandango and its competitors is evidence that a demand profit pool exists that is willing to pay more to guarantee that moviegoers can see a movie where and when they want. It's puzzling that Fandango and U.S. theater chains don't take the next logical step and allow moviegoers to reserve specific seats at a premium price rather than continuing the current scramble.

Inertia can be difficult to overcome. When it comes to pricing, businesses are often wary of changing a proven practice—even when they know they are sacrificing profits—for fear of making an even more expensive error.

A few years ago we worked with a division of a commercial printer that found itself trapped in a classic price squeeze and didn't know how to escape, because the only response it knew just made the situation worse. Like many businesses, this printer segmented its customers based on industry verticals, such as retailing, banking, and credit cards, as well as by the size of each customer. This model had worked in the past—but times had changed. For one thing, the entire printing industry was struggling with overcapacity, which was driving prices down. To make matters worse, our printer had a network of high-quality, high-capability, and relatively high-cost printing plants. And they had to be kept busy.

The printer was also blessed with a very talented sales force, but frustratingly, almost every sale they were now making involved some sort of price cutting. Worse, many of these price concessions made the deals unprofitable, but they had to be done to maintain enough volume to keep the printing plants running.

In other words, the printer was doing everything right, but was getting killed by plummeting prices. The situation had gotten so bad, and the mounting losses so huge, that the printer was seriously considering divesting this division even though it would mean a significant loss.

Before that took place, the printer decided to take one last shot—and invited us in to see if we could locate a new source of profit. As it happens, we found *two* potentially attractive demand profit pools.

One of these attractive targets was comprised mostly of retailers who were highly dependent on catalogs to drive sales. These retailers had valuable brands that required a quality presentation, and they did not want that image tarnished by a cheap-looking catalog. Just as important, the colors of the products these retailers sold—apparel, bedding, table linens, and furniture—had to be reproduced precisely so as not to disappoint consumers when the products they ordered actually arrived. Failure to do so could lead to costly returns. What we found was that these customers were willing to pay a premium for a guarantee of the kind of high-quality catalogs and accurate color reproduction our client was uniquely able to deliver.

If this first group of customers was concerned with quality, the second we found was obsessed with *time*. These were retailers whose entire business depended on getting their catalogs out in time for the holidays, to introduce products for a new season, or to promote a new store opening. These folks were willing to pay a premium for timely delivery, because any failure would be catastrophic. For them, our printer's national footprint of printing plants meant its catalogs could be printed and distributed around the country or within a specific geographic region rapidly, on time, and with lower distribution costs.

The identification of these two demand profit pools proved to be a turning point for the printer. It was able to precisely align its offerings and its marketing with these two high-profit customer groups; then, armed with both these tools and its new insights, the sales force started winning business without slashing prices. In the end, sales began setting new records—at premium prices. The reason was simple: as we've found with many clients across industries, salespeople typically spend their time where they generate the most volume. That's because most are compensated on commissions tied to volume, rather than profit. Shifting the framework and the incentive structure to a focus on the most profitable customers will increase sales margins almost instantly.

The once-troubled division quickly returned to profitability, posting strong double-digit sales gains, and within one year, saw profitability jump 30 percent. And it all occurred in an industry plagued with chronic oversupply and falling prices.

MAXIMIZING VALUE

Principle #2: Value = Benefits/Price.

Once you have identified and characterized your demand profit pools, the secret to optimizing pricing opportunities is to maximize the value you deliver to consumers in those target pools.

What is that "value"? From your customers' perspective, value has two components:

- The benefits delivered

- The price paid to obtain them

Businesses in turn have two options for increasing the value customers perceive for their offerings: either increase the benefits delivered in the numerator, or lower the price charged in the denominator. Since the latter means cutting into profits, smart companies focus on the former—and that in turn means they must develop an in-depth understanding of both the rational and emotional benefits sought by their most profitable customer groups.

How do you do that? You get to know them, you get inside their heads, and you *ask* them what they want. And then you research some more, because most consumers don't entirely know what they want or why they want it. *Rational benefits* are generally the tangible, measurable benefits delivered by a product and service. These are usually easy to discover and characterize. For example, for an automobile, they could include horsepower, gas mileage, crash-test safety ratings, "green" impact, and the number of passengers it can accommodate. By comparison, the *emotional benefits* of an automobile may include a cool design, a greater feeling of power, freedom, safety, or affiliation with a marquee that promotes prestige.

If human beings made purchasing decisions based only on rational benefits, business would be a whole lot easier (and very boring). In truth, customer choices are never entirely rational, as the growing body of behavioral economics data have shown. Even when we think we are being entirely objective in making a choice, all sorts of hidden and unconscious forces are at work on our decision.

As they've improved their understanding of the complex buying process, companies have begun to add to their offerings a range of emotional benefits to their products and services. One of these is branding, of course. That's why companies pour billions of dollars per year into brand building; it creates a bond with consumers that is very hard to break.

We use a simple test to determine the strength of a company's brand: how much of a premium does that brand command in the market? Strong brands command significant premiums—think Apple, airline mileage credit cards, Boar's Head bologna, and, of course, Bud Light Lime—while products that can only earn commodity prices represent, at best, weak brands.

And how do you build a strong brand? Look at the history of any really strong brand and you'll inevitably discover that they did so by effectively delivering against the key rational and emotional benefits sought by their highest-profit customers—even if they didn't explicitly pursue that strategy. Once they captured those pools, these companies were able to command a price premium based on the incremental benefits they provided, while still delivering a compelling value to those target customers. In other words:

(Perceived) Value = (Perceived) Benefits/Price.

To its customers, a $400,000 Rolls-Royce is a great value for the price.

We're not just talking about high ticket items, either. Think back to our Bud Light Lime case. As you'll recall, the team had discovered a previously unidentified emerging demand for a sweeter taste in beers. From there, the team developed a new product specifically designed to address the needs of this newly discovered sweeter taste group.

Field taste tests convinced Anheuser-Busch that it had a winner on its hands with Bud Light Lime. The big question now was: how to price it? There was a lot of pressure in the company, based on historic precedent, the expectations of the sales force, and concern about retailers, to simply price the new product at exactly the same price as all other Bud Light six-packs. That's how A-B had always done it, and so had all of its big competitors. The unwritten rule was: *maintain the same prices within a product line.*

But given those newly uncovered demand insights, as well as the quantitative models we had developed, we were convinced that the profit-optimizing price for Bud Light Lime—that is, the price at which both volume and margin were optimized—was a full *one dollar* higher than the other premium six-packs. That's what we mean by "pricing to demand," by pricing to the high-profit demand profit pools.

To its great credit, Anheuser-Busch chose to break with precedent and go with the higher price. We've already told you what happened: Bud Light Lime was the most successful new product launch in the food and beverage industry in 2008,[5] becoming one of the fastest growing beers introduced in the last thirty years. And it did so even at the higher price. The result was significant new incremental profits for Anheuser-Busch and the Bud Light family.

In the end, by pricing to demand profit pools rather than entire markets, Anheuser-Busch got the hat trick: it increased volume, prices *and* profits.

MAKING A DIFFERENCE

Principle #3: Meaningful differentiation is the key to pricing power.

We need to explain what "differentiation" means in this context. It is what consumers say they want from you. How do you determine that? You go to your target high-profit consumers and *ask* them: "Is this product (or service) sufficiently different to you in meaningful ways from what is being offered by competitors?"

This may seem like a simple question, but its implications are absolutely astounding. The Stern Stewart research firm has determined that if your customer believes that your product is both meaningfully relevant and highly differentiated, your margins go up *50 percent* faster, your profits go up more than *200 percent* faster, and your market capitalization also goes up more than *200 percent* faster than it does for competitors who have not successfully created relevant, differentiated offers.[6] Do you know of any other corporate activity that consistently yields these kinds of numbers? Truly, differentiation is the difference between industry winners and losers.

It also follows that one of the most effective and simple metrics for pricing is to go out and actually test the marketplace for the relevance and differentiation of your products.

What differences do you test for? Probably more than you know exist. Companies differentiate by brand, benefits, experience, packaging or pack types, perception, emotional benefits, warranties, services, distribution channels, size, appearance, safety, buying channels, speed of delivery, and on and on. Spend some morning pondering how many ways you and your products are different from your competitors and their products—and you'll quickly fill a whiteboard or two.

There are so many avenues for differentiation that it's a wonder so many companies fail to use them to their advantage. The business world is filled with companies that have built great products and services that have then failed to earn their due profits because they have failed to drive their differences and thus earn pricing power. Conversely, most great business empires have been built on meaningful differentiation: Federal Express, McDonald's, Amazon, Southwest Airlines.

Differentiation is not a new concept. Adam Smith discussed it 250 years ago in *The Wealth of Nations*.[7] There, he correctly observed that products that could be easily substituted would only be able to realize commodity prices set by the market, while products that were "non-substitutable" (that is, differentiated) could command price premiums as they can't be readily replaced.

Driving meaningful differentiation, especially when it is targeted at your most profitable demand profit pools, is a prerequisite for earning price premiums. It also builds a strong barrier to competition for those price premiums; a competitor can only drive down your price premiums if it can offer a strong substitute to your offerings in your high-profit demand profit pools. But that is very hard to do on what is essentially your home turf.

Discovering demand is a dynamic process. Even the smartest companies tend to get into ruts, continuing to differentiate their products or services in ways that worked in the past. For that reason, every six months you need to revisit your product differentiation. The best way to do that is through an exercise in which all of your product's features are on the table, you develop a set of new hypotheses for how they can be made different from the competition, and then you test those hypotheses for validity. After all, part of the definition of innovation is *novel*—and if you aren't in a perpetual search for the novel in every part of your business, you will never change.

GOOD, BETTER, BEST

Principle #4: Build and manage a "good, better, best" price trade-up architecture.

"Good, better, best," the marketing/price technique by which customers and consumers are shown a range of purchasing options and given the opportunity to make their own buying decision based on their own unique calculus of price versus performance versus quality, is most often found in the retail world. But we have determined that it is a powerful pricing tool in almost every business. That's because it has proven to be an easy way for consumers and customers to understand the price they want to pay and the level of benefits they will receive in return. Since that is the heart of the purchasing decision, anything that can throw the process into strong relief is very useful.

If you still think "good, better, best" is a technique best used for very distinctive products that feature a wide spectrum of materials and performance, such as carpeting, shop tools, or vacuum cleaners, consider the following case study about the least likely candidate for this kind of pricing differentiation: staplers.

You may well ask yourself, how can you differentiate something as simple and pedestrian as a stapler? That's what the management at Swingline, the best-known stapler brand, asked as well. The difference was that for these managers, the question wasn't an idle philosophical inquiry. Rather, it was asked with the real concern that the entire stapler category was at risk of becoming commoditized. Consumers and retailers were effectively saying (as you may have, just now), "They're just staplers, who cares? Aren't staplers all the same?"

In 2002, when Swingline brought us in, the company had been experiencing flat to declining growth and eroding margins for several years.[8] Retail consolidation and the emergence of office superstores were squeezing margins, and private label competition (once again from the superstores) was growing significantly, cutting into revenues.

One indication of the growing commodity mind-set sweeping the category was that a growing number of retailers were telling Swingline that henceforth they planned to focus on staplers in the $5 to $15 range, and drop altogether the more expensive models, especially the $70 to $120 electric staplers that had almost no sales. Were this to become standard behavior across the office supply market, it would be devastating to Swingline and its competitors.

As is often the case, we began by developing a unique understanding of consumer demand in the stapler category. It proved to be a lot more complex and interesting than you might expect for such an everyday item. Thanks to the demand landscape we developed, the team was able to understand the needs and motivations of the key demand profit pools in the market, including their demographics, psychographics, behavior patterns, motivations, benefits sought, and decision criteria.

From there, the team embarked on the process of targeting. They identified two groups of super consumers (which in this case meant people who stapled every day, such as employees in company printing departments) who had unique demands for staplers. These two groups proved to be both attractive and targetable. By interviewing these super consumers, the team further uncovered several key factors with the most impact on demand—most notably "never jamming," appearance, and page capacity.

Now Swingline had identified not only its most valuable customers, but what they were looking for when buying staplers. And this understanding of both its consumers and the benefits and features they sought now empowered Swingline to rethink its new product direction, its product positioning and messaging, and ultimately, pricing.

In the near term, however, the immediate task was to convince office supply stores to continue to sell all the Swingline's. Together, we agreed that the best way to do this was through marketing, in particular educating consumers on the fact that staplers weren't just staplers. Enter "good, better, best."

Our research had found that the typical office supply store, big or small, traditionally organized its stapler shelves by brand and price point. This may have worked well for sales clerks, but from the consumers' perspective—and worse, for manufacturers like Swingline—it made finding the right stapler difficult. This difficulty was only aggravated by the fact that most consumers buy staplers infrequently—so each stapler shopping expedition is like the first time, which makes navigating the shelves even more confusing.

We set out to make that navigation not only simple and straightforward, but also educational. The new approach called for organizing the shelf by calling out the benefits different consumers sought in the most common stapler applications. In particular, Swingline introduced new signage that guided consumers to good, better, and best staplers. In this case, the signs said: for "Everyday" use (that is, the stapler found on most desks); for "Specialty" needs (such as crafts and scrapbooking); and "High Performance" (the more expensive electric staplers).

As you might imagine, most consumers had never given much thought to the fact that staplers came in grades of quality and performance. Now, on seeing those signs, they did—and we then reinforced this education by listing on each sign the products and benefits of each category. Consumers could not only see the logical progression of benefits and price points for the different types of staplers, but see them right at the point of their purchasing decision.

What happened next wasn't entirely unexpected, but it was still surprising: more and more customers we interviewed said that, given this new information, they would trade up and buy more expensive staplers.

Armed with these data, Swingline's managers asked some of their retail customers if they could test this new merchandising approach in some of their office superstores.

The test results were eye popping. Test stores using the new merchandising approach saw sales of the higher-priced, higher-margin electric staplers *double*.[9] Furthermore, overall category sales were also up significantly—both because customers were learning about new stapler benefits, and because they were able to find exactly the item they wanted. By comparison, at the "control" stores (that didn't change their merchandising approach), category sales continued to dip—in some stores dropping as much as 10 percent.[10]

As you can well imagine, Swingline's retail partners rolled out the new merchandising strategy in all of their stores as quickly as possible. In the first year, this new merchandising approach enabled Swingline to grow its market share from 61 percent to 66 percent, reversing years of decline.[11] Even more important, sales of its high-performance products—the very ones retailers were going to eliminate from their shelves—nearly doubled.[12] This trade-up also significantly improved the company's profit margins.

Swingline had managed to not only hold the line on its declining business, but actually turned it back toward growth. It bought itself time to optimize its pricing, develop a new demand strategy, revise its product portfolio, and develop its next generation of new products. And it was able to focus on these improvements from a reestablished position of category leadership.

TAKING CONTROL

Principle #5: Be a market maker, not a price taker.

Complexity is your enemy, because too much of it makes purchasing decisions harder. You've got to make it easy to say "yes." Choice delays decisions; simplification accelerates decisions, so *simplify, simplify.*

Back in college one of us (Rick) sold shoes. He was pretty good at it, about as good as all of the other salespeople in the store . . . except for one guy. This salesman always seemed to sell twice as much as the rest of us. And nobody knew why.

So one day Rick took him to lunch. And presumptuously (being young and brash) he asked him what his trick was. "Well," the guy said, "when a woman comes into the store and asks to see simple black pumps, how many do you bring out?"

"Five," Rick replied.

"Well," he said, "I bring out two—and one of them is ugly. So while your customer is still trying to figure which one of the five they want, I've already made the sale and helped two more customers."

Map this conversation large over the entire country, and you have in a nutshell the difference between a supply-driven economy and a demand-driven economy, between price takers and market makers. Too often, companies develop and deliver their products to market without ever truly understanding the demand for those products. They're like Rick stumbling out of the back room with arms filled with every kind of black pump. They take a supply-driven approach—that is, they identify what their supply can provide and then set out to force that supply into the marketplace.

As long as demand outstripped supply, this was a viable—if wasteful—strategy. You could throw just about anything on the market and assume it would get sold eventually, even if only at a severe discount. But in a demand-driven economy, taking this "armful of shoeboxes" strategy is a recipe for failure. Ultimately, it forces you into the role of *price taker*, that of a player who must accept whatever pricing is set by competitors and the marketplace.

Two things eventually happen to price takers. First, because they take a supply-driven approach, price takers invariably produce products that either deliver benefits consumers don't want or that fail to offer benefits consumers *do* want. This is at best wasteful of precious financial and human resources in a world of declining profits, and at worst a textbook way to drive away your increasingly disappointed customers.

By comparison, taking a demand-driven approach means the perpetual pursuit to understand the highest-profit customers, and the discipline to design, produce, price, and promote for those customers. In the process, the company finds itself managing its own fate and aggressively setting the agenda, rather then being perpetually on its heels, reacting (usually late and inaccurately) to the latest unanticipated assault on its business. Demand-driven businesses are *market makers*, not merely price takers; they control their fate, rather than being at the mercy of it.

Pricing for market makers also becomes less hit-or-miss and more of a systematic and quantitative process. The goal becomes to optimize product volume (as well as incorporate an understanding of underlying costs) while delivering the benefits customers have identified as desirable—thus ensuring maximum profitability. This is pricing by logic and arithmetic, not by guesses and dartboards.

PRICING IN RETAIL

Nowhere is pricing more complex than for large retailers selling thousands of product SKUs (stock-keeping units). Yet even in these complex retail businesses, there is an orderly process that can be leveraged to optimize pricing strategy.

In developing pricing strategies, retailers must consider both the *overall pricing level* (at the retail brand or store level) and how to price *within and across categories.* Let's consider the overall pricing level first. It is a function of overall retail-brand strategy. What does your brand stand for? What pricing perceptions are you trying to reinforce and how do they link to your brand strategy?

For some retailers, pricing strategy and low prices are core to their brand equity. Consumers have come to expect that prices from these retailers will always be lower. For other retailers, however, the overall brand strategy may be to offer a high-quality in-store experience or high-quality products. Overall pricing strategy and levels for this second group of retailers might be competitive on more "commodity" items, but higher (signaling higher quality) overall.

In addition to linking overall pricing levels to brand strategy, retailers also need to account for geographic differences, in both demand for the retailer's products and services and competitive intensity.

Consider, for example, an outdoor sporting goods retailer that has stores in many different geographical locations, some urban and others rural. As you might imagine, demand for this retailer's products tends to be highest in the more rural lake regions, where more outdoor sporting activities take place. In addition, competitive intensity is actually lowest in these areas. Thus, the retailer has the opportunity to systematically price higher in these higher-demand, less-competitive areas. If it fails to do so, it will be leaving money on the table.

When pricing within and across categories, retailers often struggle with strategies at the category level. That is, should the strategy be

"Every Day Low Price" (EDLP), hi-lo, or somewhere in between? If hi-lo, how should the item be promoted?

Over the years, we have worked with retailers to develop a process that answers these questions for them, resulting in a set of unified and coordinated pricing actions across categories. Critical to activating this process is to view the offering as a *portfolio of categories, not just a set of individual one-off categories.* Similar to investments in a portfolio, the key is to keep in mind that not all categories are created equal; rather, some categories are "worth" more than others.

Still, every category has a role to play. The trick is to determine what role each category plays. In developing roles for categories, most retailers consider how much revenue or profit a category generates and then use that information to develop category strategies. While this is a good start, it misses some of the key demand drivers. A far superior strategy for the retailer is to better understand—and leverage—the importance of the category *to the consumer*, not just the retailer. To do that requires answering several questions:

- Is the category big (total market demand)?

- Is it growing?

- Is it frequently shopped (relative to other categories)?

- Does the category drive retail choice?

- What is the retailer's share of wallet or penetration? How does that compare to other retailers? Do consumers view this as a strength of the retailer or a relative area of weakness?

Once you know the relative importance of each category, you can prioritize all categories. Category prioritization can help you to align price and promotional investment allocation along with other critical decisions such as assortment, shelf space, ad space, and merchandising. Experience has shown us that the top 30 percent of the categories drive about 50 percent of the profit (these are usually the categories that drive retail choice); the next 30 percent of the categories drive about 30 percent of the profit; and the bottom 40 percent of the categories drive about 20 percent of the profit.[13] That's a valuable piece of information when determining the role each category should play.

But simply prioritizing the categories does not give a merchant guidance on how best to manage their categories. Just because that merchant knows that he or she has a priority category does not mean that the merchant knows how best to invest in that category or what type of pricing strategy to employ. To do that, we need to leverage an in-depth and proprietary understanding of how consumers interact with those categories.

• *Elasticity* What role does price play? Is the category elastic? What's important in evaluating price elasticity is not the absolute elasticity, but the relative price elasticity. Suppose salty snacks and infant formula are both top priority categories for a retailer. Now consider that salty snacks are relatively more elastic than infant formula. Knowing this enables the retailer to invest more in salty snacks.

• *Pricing* Is price a driver of retailer choice? Does it help drive overall retailer price perceptions? Milk (conventional, nonorganic) is a category that will help to set price perception and consumer expectations for a store. Grocery retailers might offer hot prices on other items, but if they are off on milk, they will not get credit for the lower prices that they offer in other categories.

Moreover, the retailer must consider not only the role that price plays, but also the benefits sought when shopping for the category.

• *Brand* How brand-loyal are consumers? Are consumers willing to switch brands?

• *Variety* Is the category inherently variety-seeking in nature, so that the consumer rotates through a series of products? Or do consumers tend to stick with the same product every time?

• *Novelty* What are the consumer expectations regarding product innovation and newness? Does the assortment change frequently? Should it?

So what does a merchant or category manager do with this information? Consider carbonated soft drinks (CSDs). This category is highly price elastic, drives retail choice, and is brand-driven, meaning that consumers tend to be pretty loyal to one brand and are more likely to choose their retailer based on whether it has their favorite brand of soda on sale. If the merchant knows this information, he or she can make sure that big CSDs are consistently on sale, offering deep discounts to drive consumers to the store.

Similarly, consider the kids' cereals category, which is more inherently variety-seeking in nature. Consumers are less loyal to a single brand and more likely to rotate through a series of brands. The category is also somewhat elastic, as consumers do buy more when the category is promoted. Using the information, a merchant can facilitate the variety-seeking nature of the category by offering mix and match promotions.

The lesson is that no matter how complex and extensive the challenge, it is still possible to implement a rational, profit-maximizing pricing strategy driven not by supply, but consumer demand.

STAYING UNIQUE

If there is one overarching message that you should take from this chapter, it is that *no product or service ever needs to be a commodity unless you let it become one.*

In every category there exists a core group of consumers who are positively engaged with that category, and who are not only motivated to obtain certain of its products and services, but are willing to pay a premium price for them. The way for your company to win is to find those customers, optimize your product offering around them, and enjoy the opportunity to be a market maker with a price premium earned through optimized alignment with demand.

We'll finish this chapter with the story of a major pharmaceutical company that took just this path: from taking a demand approach, to leveraging the insights it gained about demand for one of its over-the-counter (OTC) products, to fully revamping its pricing strategy and enjoying unprecedented market dominance and profitability.

In 2007, faced with increasing price pressures from branded and private label competitors, as well as low levels of consumer loyalty across the category, this company decided, with considerable fanfare, to restage one of its key strategic brands.

Unfortunately, this restaging fell short of the company's expectations. In turn, that forced the company to reexamine its entire brand strategy—not least, its pricing. Management wanted to increase revenues and profits for the brand by optimizing this pricing strategy, all while reducing the brand's growing reliance on deep-discount promotions.

This last, the discounting, was becoming a serious concern. The company's leading product SKUs had become locked into regular promotions at $6.99. These promotions were now so frequent that consumers had no incentive to trade up the price/size continuum within the brand.

As we showed the company, breaking this discounting pattern was not as simple as merely ending the program. That would only disappoint customers and potentially drive some of them away. Rather, the company had to develop a complete understanding of demand in the category.

As part of that process, we took a closer look at the company's current pricing strategy. What we found surprised the company as much as it did us. What everyone thought was a comparatively straightforward pricing program proved to be surprisingly complex. In turned out that the brand maintained *seven* distinct price points spread across *twenty-seven* SKUs.[14] This reality was way too complex for consum-

ers to have to think about. Moreover, the deep and inconsistent promotional activity across the product line distorted the price/value
equation for consumers, which resulted in even more confusion. The
current approach was difficult for consumers to navigate and provided
almost no incentive for consumers to trade up to larger pack sizes or
new/specialty formulas. Basically, they just waited for the $6.99 dis-
count package and made their purchase.

Working with company management, we suggested a new strategy:
simplify the pricing strategy to feature two key promotional blocks,
and improve incentives to trade up within and across product formula-
tions. Given the ongoing promotional activity in the category, the net
result for retailers would be a nearly 20 percent increase in price.[15]

Meanwhile, for consumers, removing the very low promoted prices
allowed for a more logical and lower price per pill for the larger package sizes. This approach helped the company gain new users, while
simultaneously encouraging existing users to both trade up and try
new formulas more tailored to their needs. At the end of the day, the
new approach simplified the confusing promotions and specialty-pack
sizes that were originally developed for promotions, but now cluttered
the shelf and inhibited trade-up. The result? Let's look at each of the
stakeholders in turn.

Consumers finally had a clear price/value equation that incentivized
existing users to trade up to larger pack sizes in order to realize lower
per-pill prices. They were also guided to premium sub-brands more
tailored to their needs but until now had been lost in the noise and
clutter. With the category easier to navigate, new users entered the category and gained the health benefits it provided. The simpler approach
also gave consumers fewer reasons to switch, making them more loyal
to the brand.

Retailers, as might be expected, after escaping a dependency on
discounting, improved their margins. They also became less reliant on
price promotions and simplified their category pricing overall. They
also enjoyed the addition of new customers for the product line.

The *manufacturer*, our pharmaceutical client, increased revenues, improved margins, reduced trade spending, and generally simplified its pricing structure to two key price points. So successful was this new strategy that the profits gained from the changed pricing approach were equivalent to launching a successful new brand, but with none of the expenses attached to such a launch.

For everyone involved, this was a very big win.

SMART PRICING

Successful pricing strategies generate customer loyalty and trade-up while driving competitive insulation.

What separates pricing-strategy successes from suboptimal pricing programs is that the successes inevitably show a deep and differentiated understanding of demand. To realize maximum price premiums, you must truly understand both the category and the most profitable segments of demand in that category. Actionable insights on demand are the foundation for optimizing pricing strategies.

Understanding demand writes the rules of engagement; pricing is how you win the game. It is the payoff for all your preparation.

We'll close by repeating the rules of pricing one more time, to underscore their importance:

1. Price to demand profit pools, not to markets.
2. Leverage the value equation: Value = Benefits/Price.
3. Drive differentiation that is critical to pricing power.
4. Build and manage a logical "good, better, best" price trade-up architecture.
5. Be a market maker, not a price taker.

Build them into your business. And every six months hold a pricing review to revisit them—and to make sure you aren't missing any chances for differentiation. In pricing, the only constant is change.

PART III

EXECUTION

SEVEN

ORGANIZING TO WIN

Aligning Your Company for Success

It has been said that the ultimate job of a leader is to get people to follow.

But after observing leaders in dozens of companies over the past thirty years, we've come to realize that the real question to be asked is not just, can a leader get people to follow him, but, to follow him *where*?

In this chapter we are going to briefly turn away from the immediate problems of new products, new markets, and pricing—and look at the big picture. In particular, you need to ask yourself: *Does my company have a simple—and easily understood—plan for how it will succeed?* and *Does everyone in the company understand that plan and their role within it?*

Successful companies, especially if they stay successful, always have just such a plan for winning, and regularly revisit it. Great companies (the ones that stay on top of their markets for decades) align their internal operations, from the boardroom to the receptionist, to be in total support of that plan. And they regularly communicate that message to their employees.

We call these external/internal strategies the "thesis for winning" and "mental models." Let's look at them in turn, and then at how they connect.

As the years have gone by, it has become absolutely clear to us that all truly outstanding leaders have a thesis for winning—that is, a set of individual principles, each in itself important, that when taken together represent the strategy to take and the pathway to follow for that business to win. It is what Ed Liddy, former chairman and CEO of Allstate Insurance, calls "The Theory of the Game."[1]

Liddy speaks with authority and experience, because his own thesis for winning across his eight years at the top of Allstate produced remarkable results. He was intent on driving profitability as a percentage of sales—and the results are there for all to see. When Liddy became CEO in 1999, company revenues were $27 billion and net income $2.7 billion.[2] When he retired in 2006, revenues had increased to $36 billion, but profits had skyrocketed to almost $5 billion.[3]

Few leaders have accomplished such remarkable growth in a company's profit-to-sales ratio. And Liddy credits the success, in part, to giving Allstate a strong thesis for winning. As Liddy describes it, he had three elements in his thesis:

1. *Deliver better service* at all levels of Allstate, starting with their agents.

2. *Deliver better pricing* based on the lifetime value of the customers.

3. *Communicate constantly* to Allstate's 12,000 agents the importance of good service in attracting and retaining customers and to its millions of insureds that Allstate puts its "good hands" commitment to customer service foremost.

Needless to say, Allstate had numerous long-term growth strategies as well as short-term programs to execute these elements. But ultimately, it was Liddy's thesis for winning that ensured that everyone in the company understood what the company was trying to accomplish, which channeled and aligned all of its programs into a single-minded pursuit of victory, and which showed employees how, in the end, All-

state would win versus its very considerable competitors. "It v
theory of the game" says Liddy. "It was what we had to do to win in the
property and casualty business."[4]

BELIEFS AND OBJECTIVES

Here is our definition of the thesis for winning: *Management's set of
beliefs and objectives, which, taken in combination, establishes the basis
on which a corporation intends to win versus its competitors.*

Now let's take a closer look at what makes up those beliefs and
objectives:

1. Realism A thesis for winning must be grounded in facts versus
opinions; real actions versus being merely theoretical; pragmatic
versus ideal. It must reflect your company's real capabilities, not those
you wish it had. And it must be grounded in the real-life facts of your
industry, your customers, and your competitors.

2. Belief You have to believe that now or in the near future you will
win with this plan because it drives distinct competitive advantages.
Why do you believe that? There are many factors that can convince
you, from the rigorous tools of analytics, to experience, to the "gut
feel" of intuition.

3. Measurement You can create metrics to track your thesis vis-à-vis
your competitors. If you cannot measure the performance of your
thesis for winning, then it is unrealistic.

4. Resources You can allocate resources to your thesis. If you can't
back your plan with capital and people, it is unrealistic.

5. Demand Your thesis for winning is grounded in the knowledge that
at each point, and with every new initiative, it will uniquely satisfy customer demand.

6. Differentiation Your thesis for winning must be differentiated from your competitors'. As no two companies are exactly alike, even if they are competing in the same market, so, too, should no two theses be alike.

7. Ratification You must ensure both that your employees are aligned with your thesis for winning, and your customers are in support of it. This, in turn, means that your thesis must not be secret or closely held by only top management. Rather, it should be broadcast to every stakeholder to assure that everyone has the same goals and expectations.

It is crucial to underscore that unlike, say, the laws of physics, there are no fixed rules for a thesis for winning, nor is that thesis permanent. Rather, its objectives and beliefs should be consistent with your analysis of your industry and your position in it and be realistic for your organization. A great thesis for winning evolves with time as the company, its employees and management, its customers, and even the culture itself, changes.

PLAYING TO WIN

The thesis for winning is part fact-based, part philosophy-based, and part strategy-based—but it is all about how to win. No successful leader can rely wholly on making decisions one at a time.

Take football. While a team must participate in all parts of the game—offense, defense, special teams—highly successful coaches determine in which part of the game their team is going to dominate. The result is a series of questions in the form of a decision tree:

- Do we dominate in offense or defense?

- If offense, will we focus on the running game or the passing game?

- If passing, will it be the "West Coast offense" of short, disciplined passes, or the long game, which uses deep passes to stretch the field to open up for the running game?

Each answer generates a new either/or question. And the list of questions goes on and on: thus, if you choose a West Coast offense, then you have to ask if you have the right player at every position or whether you will need to trade for some of them. Are the players you need available? Can you afford them? How do you deal with the weaknesses of this offense? How do you deal with the different defenses other teams will put up against you?

All coaches have different game plans for different games, depending on whom they are playing and other factors. But every *great* coach also has a thesis for winning; that framework through which he thinks not only about individual games but entire seasons—and how to win far more often than his competitors. And it goes beyond that, because the coach also uses this thesis as a filter for recruiting assistant coaches who not only agree with the plan but also understand how their part of the game dovetails with and supports the larger plan. The same is true for players, recruited not only on how well their style of play fits into the overall plan but also for their ability to understand their individual role in the bigger picture.

Bill Walsh, the famed San Francisco 49er's coach who invented the West Coast offense, was a master of the thesis for winning. Inheriting a consistently losing team, he developed a long-term plan that he knew would result in at least one horrible season as he recruited and traded for the right players to execute it. In a game characterized by a tight focus on next week's game, Walsh looked out five years ahead—then systematically executed a complex and multitiered thesis for winning that included:

1. Infrastructure Recruit and train the right on-field and coaching talent to execute the West Coast offense—and plan to take at least three years building it.

2. Strategy Plan for the entire season, not just the next game. Incorporate pacing, home versus travel games, and the styles of the opposing teams.

3. Tactics Enter each game with a distinct plan, and all other factors being equal, do not deviate from that plan, even under the pressure of events.

4. Contingencies Expect the unexpected, such as an injured key player. Be flexible enough to adapt your game plan to these game-changing events.

At the time, the actual application of Walsh's thesis for winning was so rare and unexpected that many observers (including other coaches) scratched their heads at his seemingly inexplicable behavior. For example, there was the famous clipboard on which Walsh reportedly scripted the first thirty offensive plays of the game. Only later did Walsh explain that what appeared to be programmatic and rigid was in fact just the opposite: he had scripted the plays ahead of time to exhibit an unpredictability, because Walsh knew that unscripted and in the pressure of the game, he would lose his creativity and become *more* predictable.

Another inexplicable move (at the time) was Walsh's decision to make Joe Montana—a sixth-round draft choice—the 49ers' starting quarterback.[5] By most lights, Montana—skinny, comparatively weak arm—was a poor choice for the NFL. But what Walsh had seen in a famous Cotton Bowl game when Montana was still at Notre Dame was a fierce, competitive intelligence that seemed to grow more acute under pressure. Walsh made a similar decision about halfback Roger Craig, who would have been mediocre with most offenses but who had the "soft" hands of an excellent pass receiver. And in Ronnie Lott, Walsh found a defensive player whose aggressiveness was balanced by a deep commitment to team leadership.

Meanwhile Walsh, recognizing that the West Coast offense placed team over individual and required almost ballet-like coordination, didn't hesitate to trade away players—even superstars—who didn't fit into the "system." So well-thought-out was this thesis for winning that

Coach Walsh could actually recite by memory the dozens of entries and subentries of the thesis in outline form.

In this way, Walsh systematically built a team that, by traditional measures, would have been second tier, but that was perfectly aligned to his thesis for winning. The rest is history: four Super Bowl victories (the last a year after Walsh retired), and with many of its players in the Hall of Fame, the Niners of the Walsh era are now considered one of the greatest teams in NFL history.

NO ONE BEST WAY

Perhaps the most celebrated winning thesis in modern business history is that of Hewlett-Packard under its founders. This story alone is worth reading. But there is also a second narrative here as well, because HP has managed to succeed *twice*, each time with a radically different winning thesis. It is a reminder that no single such plan is right for different companies in the same business, or even the same company at different moments in time.

Intellectually, we understand why this must be so, but emotionally we often do not. There is a tendency in human beings to assume that there is a one best way to do almost anything. This notion goes back at least to Plato, who held that the things of this world were, in fact, merely flawed manifestation of underlying ideal versions.

This notion that there is a single best solution to any problem can still be found everywhere in the business world, from Six Sigma to libraries of "best practices."

There is, of course, nothing wrong with doing the best job you can in order to achieve the very highest levels of success. That's what business competition is all about. But to suggest that there is only one true path to that success, or that there is a single, perfect solution, can often paralyze a company as it spends more time looking for that ideal strategy than actually executing it.

In our experience, there is no perfect answer to how companies win; rather, there is an array of different paths to success, and they can be traveled in a multitude of different ways. What is important is that whatever thesis for winning a company chooses, it must first be congruent with the company's internal culture—and where it is not, either the plan itself, or the company's internal culture, must be modified to achieve that congruence.

The history of Hewlett-Packard, the world's largest technology company ($115 billion in annual revenues[6]) is a classic example of how one company can pursue radically different plans at different times and still emerge consistently victorious.

THE HP WAY

Hewlett-Packard (HP) had the most famous start in American business history. Two 1930s graduates of Fred Terman's electronics lab at Stanford University decided that they wanted to start a company together, and to build it near the university in order to get Terman's ongoing advice. David Packard and his new bride had just rented a house in downtown Palo Alto, and Bill Hewlett (for the moment still a bachelor) had moved into a shed out back. The property also had a garage—now a national historic site—where Bill and Dave set up some workbenches and went to work.

After a few failed starts, Hewlett and Packard settled on one of Bill's graduate school products—a sound wave generator called an "audio oscillator"—and set about manufacturing it. They named it the model 200A because that seemed like a big number, and priced it at $54.40 after an event in U.S. history.[7] Sales were slim until Walt Disney, needing to manage the audio track in the movie *Fantasia*, ordered eight—and Hewlett-Packard was on its way.

For the next decade, the company struggled, not least because Hewlett was called off to World War II and Packard had to manage the rapidly growing company and its increasing number of military contracts. Hewlett's wartime experiences taught him the power of perpetual technological innovation; the overextended Packard learned how productive people can be if they are entrusted to make their own decisions. Combined, these two business philosophies produced the most admired (and influential) corporate culture of the twentieth century.

But one ingredient was missing. It came after the war, during that brief economic downturn between the war boom and the fifties. Facing a collapse in orders, Hewlett-Packard was forced to lay off some of the same employees who had held the company together just a few years before. Packard found the experience so painful that he swore it would never happen again—and during the next forty years of Bill and Dave's leadership of the company, it never did.

By the early 1950s, Hewlett-Packard had developed a powerful business strategy, its thesis for winning: it was only to compete in new technology markets where it could capture market dominance and stay ahead of the competition through continual innovation and superior quality—and because of these factors, be able to charge a higher price and enjoy the industry's largest profit margins. By holding to this plan, HP was able to not only outrun its larger competitors such as IBM and DEC, but also stay ahead of all but the most dynamic new tech start-up companies.

The result was that during the fifties, sixties, and seventies, Hewlett-Packard was arguably the world's most innovative company, producing a roll call of landmark products from atomic clocks to scientific calculators—and in the process, creating huge new markets around each of them. It was only when the company deviated from its thesis for winning that HP stumbled. For example, it went into the oscilloscope market after Tektronix pioneered the business, spent a quarter-century chasing the Oregon company, and in the end always ran a distant second. It was only in minicomputers, where HP arrived late after IBM, DEC, and Data General, that Hewlett-Packard ever violated its thesis for winning and ultimately succeeded—but it took decades, and arguably HP's final victory came because of other factors that *were* part of its evolving thesis for winning.

Historians who have studied HP during this era have all agreed that the success of HP's strategy was critically dependent on the company's internal culture. This culture was called the "HP Way," and like all great corporate cultures, it was not easy to explain, but employees had internalized it so completely that they intuitively knew it when they saw it.

The HP Way is generally agreed to have three parts:[8]

1. A Climate of Innovation Everything about HP during this era was organized around the perpetual invention of new and breakthrough products that not only outdistanced the competition, but rendered the competition irrelevant by creating fundamentally new businesses. The obverse of this is that whenever company products began to show signs of overcompetition, slowing innovation, or price commoditization, they were abandoned—even if, like the HP-35 calculator, they were synonymous with the company.

2. A Culture of Trust Though more common today, HP was revolutionary at the time for driving decision making *down* through the organization to the person who was closest to the matter. This would be later characterized as an "inverted pyramid" organization. The company underscored this through a series of celebrated employee-oriented programs, pioneering or popularizing such innovations as profit sharing, employee stock options, catered morning and afternoon coffee breaks, Friday beer busts, and most famously, employee flextime.

3. Management by Objective David Packard and his senior management first devised MBO at an executive retreat in 1957. At its peak, HP operated on a set of six objectives: profit, customers, field of interest, growth, employees, organization, and citizenship. The details of these objectives were revisited and revised by the company every few years, but the core objectives themselves remained the same, and in the same order of priority. Implicit in these objectives was Hewlett-Packard's long-term thesis for winning, the strategy for how the company was going to compete and win.

Once the thesis for winning was in place, Hewlett-Packard established its mental model—which became a reality when HP's employees universally believed in that strategy and became aligned at every level. The extraordinary success of HP was, in an important way, realized because the mental model enabled the achievement of HP's thesis for winning.

So deeply did the employees of Hewlett-Packard, from the chairman to the janitor, internalize the HP Way that it became largely self-enforcing. During the recession of 1974, in perhaps the greatest test of the HP Way, the company was once again faced with layoffs. Instead, management proposed, and employees accepted, the "nine day fortnight," in which *every* HPer worked ten days but was only paid for nine. No jobs were lost.

It is not surprising, then, to learn that sociologists surveying HP employees later that decade were astounded to find that the company had the highest levels of loyalty and morale ever measured in a large company. At the same time, HP was growing as fast as any big company in high-tech history. That combination led one well-known business author to declare Hewlett-Packard during that era to have been "the world's greatest company."

FINDING A NEW WAY

The HP Way survived Hewlett's and Packard's retirements in the late 1970s, and in fact, the company continued its impressive growth for nearly a decade. But Bill and Dave's successors increasingly had trouble either matching the company's operating philosophy with their own personalities, or making HP's traditional strategic approach congruent with the changing nature of the marketplace. Employees increasingly began to feel as if the company was beginning to lose its way.

They were right. By 1990, the company's sales and profits flattened,[9] and in the face of hot, young companies like Apple and Yahoo, HP began to look old and out of touch. This set the stage for what has been dubbed "The Great Return," in which Bill and Dave, now both old men, came back to the company, reasserted the HP Way, stripped away old product lines, and established for their company a new thesis. By the time they left again, now for the last time, Hewlett-Packard was revitalized—and, briefly, the fastest growing Fortune 50 company ever.

But it wasn't to last. The Great Return was a reminder of both the greatness of Hewlett and Packard as business leaders, and how much HP depended on their personalities. For the next fifteen years, the company went through a succession of CEOs, two of them promoted from within, the third a hired corporate superstar. But each in his or her own way failed to restore HP to its old glory.

The internally promoted executives understood the company's internal dynamics, its resources and capabilities, and the importance of the HP Way, but they never constructed an effective thesis for winning. The outsider superstar *did* find a winning strategy, but the plan she devised to execute it was so antithetical to the HP corporate culture—that is, it so failed the thesis requirements for "congruence" and "ratification"—that it actually set off a mutiny by the company's employee-shareholders. Clearly, she never came close to establishing an internal mental model that would have enabled the company to achieve what turned out to be a successful thesis for winning. In the end, the superstar was fired for want of a mental model.

What was that otherwise-workable thesis for winning? It was to restore HP to its former glory by turning it into a fast-moving, price-competitive manufacturer. But to do that meant driving out the HP Way and putting in its place a more top-down organization for faster decision making. HP's employees, however, felt differently—and the result was a kind of corporate civil war.

Enter Mark Hurd, the new Hewlett-Packard CEO. He had made a name for himself at NCR as a tough and disciplined chief executive who ruthlessly cut costs and nonproductive product lines and fought competitors with manufacturing, quality, and competitive pricing.

In the years to come, and as HP again returned to its winning ways, some observers suggested that all new management had really done was to execute based on the strategy of their immediate predecessor. There is, in fact, a lot of truth to that. What they did was streamline the company and its products, focusing largely on the personal computer, enterprise server, and imaging (printers, scanners, digital photography) businesses, and then relentlessly cut costs. It was a risky move—HP was, after all, proposing to win in a market (PCs) that was increasingly seen as becoming commoditized; another (servers) where they would ultimately face huge competitors such as Sun and Cisco; and a third, imaging, where HP would face veteran consumer electronics products makers like Canon.

But HP also had luck on its side. IBM pulled out of the PC business, the Asian PC makers began to abandon the market, and chief competitor Dell suddenly seemed to lose its way. Meanwhile, Sun began to die and Cisco decided for the time being to work with HP rather than against it. And in imaging, HP simply beat the competition with better, cheaper offerings.

So if management was, in large part, executing its predecessors' strategy, why did they succeed—turning HP into history's first $100 billion tech company—where the former CEO had failed, even provoking an employee mutiny in the process?

The simple answer is that Hurd did what his predecessor had failed to do: he got both his management and the rank-and-file HP employees behind this new quality manufacturer/PC-printer dominant/price competitive thesis for winning strategy. He established a mental model internally that enabled the successful thesis for winning externally.

In this, HP was both lucky and smart. They were lucky because, thanks to all of the hirings, layoffs, retirements, and frustrations of the previous fifteen years, the HP of 2005 had very few employees who even *remembered* the HP Way. That majority who had fought his predecessor in the proxy battle had now dwindled to a small minority—and most of them were now inured to the idea that the Bill and Dave years were never coming back.

Just as important, the new HP CEO, made two brilliant public relations moves. First, he positioned himself as the opposite of his high-profile predecessor by refusing nearly all public appearances, pushing others into the limelight, and crediting his employees for the company's success. This immediately improved HP employees' trust in top management. Second, he used the first few months to pay his respects to the HP Way, honoring the company's two founders, visiting employees and company retirees, and enlisting them in the crusade to restore HP's success.

The last was particularly important because Hurd had no real plans to restore the old HP Way culture. It fit neither his temperament nor his plans for the company. Rather, his campaign was designed to earn employees' confidence that he *did* have a thesis for winning, and most of all, that he would restore the company (and by extension, its employees) to prosperity.

A focus on *success*—in manufacturing, in quality, in price competitiveness, and most of all in market dominance—became the new catchword for Hewlett-Packard. And HPers, suddenly feeling job security, enjoying salary raises, and watching their stock value climb—even as the rest of the computer industry stumbled—found a new reason to be loyal employees of Hewlett-Packard. They ratified the new plan or they moved on. The same was true for senior management.

Has Hewlett-Packard been as enlightened and innovative as it had been under Bill and Dave? No. But it was at least as successful—an impressive achievement considering the sheer size of HP in 2010 and the changed nature of the competitive landscape. In 2007, Hewlett-Packard became the first IT company in history to break $100 billion in annual revenues. In 2009, it surpassed Dell to become the world's largest computer maker.[10] It is the world leader in the inkjet, laser, large format, and multifunction printers markets, number two in IT services, and the sixth largest software company. It also became the "greenest" large company in America. HP went from being a lost and increasingly moribund old technology company and, armed with a powerful thesis for winning, in just five years HP transformed into a young, aggressive, and—most of all—*winning* company again.

The lesson of the HP story is that there is no one ideal company model nor one perfect, permanent thesis for winning. Different times, different markets, and different leaders, almost always require a new winning thesis. Like the company it serves, a thesis for winning needs to *grow* and *change*. It also needs for its voice to be heard, not just outside the company but within.

It is this internal message, whose task it is to bring all employees and stakeholders into common cause, that we call the mental model.

FORGING AHEAD TOGETHER

It was late at night and we were sitting in the boardroom of one of the world's largest food companies. The empty pizza boxes in the middle of the elegant wood table suggested a casual gathering—but the group was anything but relaxed.

The conversation was about why profit margins were falling across the company, and the managers around the table were struggling to understand why they continued to miss their numbers.

Finally, the head of the sales department said, "Look, for us the problem is that we are always the last to get to our supermarket customers with our plans and programs."

The head of the marketing department, feeling threatened, responded, "That's because we don't get our final costs from the purchasing department until very late."

And the head of purchasing angrily snapped back to the head of marketing, "If you could get your info to us one month earlier, we could save 4 percent on cost of goods."

The chief marketing officer looked astonished. He announced, "You know, I've been in this job for two years, and this is the first time I've ever heard the schedule on which our purchasing department works."

Sitting at the head of the table, the president of the company listened in silence. Finally, he leaned forward and said, quietly but with a firm voice, "I now know our problem: *We're forging sideways.*"

It was that meeting that set us off on a multiyear quest to understand why the operations of some companies seem to work together smoothly, in concert, almost anticipating each other's next move, while other companies are so uncoordinated, wasting enormous amounts of time and energy, and forever working at cross-purposes.

What we discovered is that the best and most competitive companies always feature some form of this mental modeling. Here is our definition:

A mental model is the same picture in every employee's mind of how their company is going to compete and win—and their own role within that plan.

It is the commitment by the company to the notion that every function in the company—and every person within those functions—must share the same understanding of what they are going to do, and how they are going to do it, to win. And that this message must be shared with the entire company, ratified by employees, and made manifest in every move the company makes.

What is that message?

• *Here's how our market works.* It's been said that every market has its own algorithm. That is, an underlying set of rules that set its pace, its style, and its personality. These rules are rarely explicit, and almost never empirical, but everyone who works in that industry quickly learns to operate by them.

• **Here's how our competitors work.** This means understanding not only your competitor's products, target markets, and customers, but also their operating style, the means by which they compete, and their strengths and weaknesses.

• **Here's how we work.** This includes your own company's style, attitudes, and mores, how it deals with customers, shareholders, competitors, and the general public, and rules of behavior, dress, access, and communications.

• **Here's why we will win.** This is the heart of the mental model; it is the company's vision of itself as a competitor and an understanding of why its combination of products and strategy will enable it to succeed against its competitors. Not coincidentally, it is the company's thesis for winning, internalized and brought to action.

We've just recounted for you the classic story of Hewlett-Packard, a company with one of the most powerful shared mental models ever developed . . . and what happened when a new chief executive tried to impose a radically new thesis for winning on the company without addressing its poor fit with that model. The result was an employee mutiny.

A different sort of problem can occur in a company that has a strong thesis for winning but no explicitly shared mental model, as was the case with the giant food company that was forging sideways. In these cases, the company has a solid strategy, but finds itself frustratingly unable to execute that strategy, like a runner whose legs won't work together.

By comparison, almost all truly successful companies exhibit strongly shared and consistent mental models, whatever the status of their current thesis for winning. Some of these models are so powerful that they take on an iconic status to the larger public. You merely have to say the "GE Way," or mention IBM's "Think" campaign, Procter & Gamble and marketing, 3M and innovation, Apple's "cool," Mercedes-

Benz and quality, or Porsche and engineering, to evoke a whole series of mental images and emotions.

At their best, strong mental models make companies greater than the sum of their parts. They transform a company from being a collection of separate, uncoordinated operations to an integrated unit that functions together and in synchronism. When companies have achieved this level of coordination, you can actually *feel* it. It is the magic of Disney's theme parks, the complete professionalism of IBM, the distinctive environment of a Four Seasons hotel, the smooth operation of Southwest Airlines, and the consistency of any McDonald's anywhere in the world. This coordination and consistency stem from a powerful shared mental model that allows each person to understand his or her role in achieving success.

In an increasingly globalized economy, where employees will have to often operate independently in some distant corner of the planet, that shared knowledge and instinctive ability to do what is required is also a powerful competitive advantage.

THE ALIGNED COMPANY

Within most companies, each successful quarter, each winning product or service builds morale, underscores mutual respect and trust, and increases pride in the company.

In the best scenario, the mental model, cascading down through the company, aligns the organization in a single-minded pursuit of the thesis for winning. This aligned company then embarks on a virtuous cycle in which common understanding increases the chances of success, and then that success further empowers the organization's mental model.

These are the companies that become business juggernauts—like Wal-Mart a decade ago, and Apple today—that seem to accelerate away from their competitors and enjoy one business success after another.

They are typically described as a having a "winning attitude" or a "culture of success," but what they really have is a strong mental model that is neatly aligned with a shrewd thesis for winning—a nearly unbeatable combination. Indeed, the only real competitive threat they might be said to face is their own complacency with success.

By comparison, a company without a shared mental model is less a company than an aggregation of different operations, each pursuing a series of activities, and each hoping that it will win. There can be tremendous talent and innovation in these operations, but if they haven't been integrated together both physically (via compatible communications, tools, rules of behavior, etc.) and philosophically (via a mental model), the company will lack both the processes and attitudes it takes to win. It will exhibit episodic behavior, disjointed activities, and wasteful overlap. Directionless, the company will indeed be "forging sideways."

For a company's mental model to work, the CEO needs to make sure all functional heads understand its key messages, and that these messages are conveyed to department heads, and then down through the organization. Mental models don't just occur; they are created. For example, we have helped some companies create a mental model and then conducted what we call a "demand university" in which hundreds of managers are exposed to and take part in training related to that mental model. The demand university training always includes the "hows" and "whys" the company will win against its competitors. Indeed, if that message isn't conveyed, then most of the rest of the training is almost beside the point.

The mental model creates comfort for employees because they understand the larger picture and their important role within it. From that comfort springs confidence, which is the hallmark of high-performing employees and winning companies.

MOTO MENTAL MODEL

Here's another example of what we mean. A number of years ago, we were asked to give a speech to one of the world's best-known high-tech companies: Motorola Inc.

Founded in 1928, Motorola pioneered almost every major technology revolution of the next eighty years, from automobile radios to television to the transistor to the integrated circuit to the microprocessor to the cell phone. When it didn't invent one of those technologies, it was a key player in advancing the art; and when it didn't lead in an industry, it was inevitably a close second. And when Motorola didn't lead in innovation, it inevitably competed strongly with marketing and manufacturing.

As you might imagine, for a proud company with such a lustrous history, Motorola had a powerful mental model. This model was colloquialized as: *We are warring bands of 50,000 engineers.*

What this meant was that everybody in the company, but especially its engineers, were driven to be perpetual innovators—the strategy being that if every one of the company's legions of engineers was to continually work on developing new products and processes, that somewhere among those warring bands the next great tech breakthrough would emerge. And the one after that. And if the company continued to innovate, it didn't matter if one product line or another stumbled or failed . . . because waiting in the wings would be the Next Big Thing that would enable Motorola to end-run the competition into the next high-profit/fast-growing market.

It was a model that had worked for decades—and the process propelled Motorola into a company with $30 billion in annual revenues.[11] Over and over, when the company had stumbled—as it had getting its first microprocessor design to work, and in developing a follow-up product to its wildly successful Razr cell phone—it inevitably innovated its way back to success. So as you can imagine, the company was wary of any suggestion of compromising or changing the mental model that had made it rich.

The problem was that with the new century, this mental model, with its complementary thesis for winning by using innovation to bypass or bulldoze any competitive obstacle in its way, suddenly didn't serve the company the way it once had. In chips, the company was consistently losing ground to Intel—to the point where its biggest customer, Apple Computers, finally abandoned the Motorola processor and switched to Intel.[12] In cell phones, Motorola, which had all but owned the market a decade before with its StarTAC phones, was now falling far behind fast-moving competitors like Nokia and Samsung.

At an earlier time in the supply-driven economy, Motorola's mental model was appropriate and very successful. Technology moved more slowly then and there were many fewer competitors. In that day and age, engineers could create supply and go in search of demand to absorb what they had created. However, holding on to what worked in the past and not evolving their mental model now led to years of disappointing performance and upheaval for Motorola.

It wasn't that the engineers at Motorola had become any less creative. Rather, their inventions suddenly seemed out of alignment with what the market wanted—a weakness thrown into sharp relief when, even as Motorola, with some of the world's greatest telephony experts, struggled to get a new generation of phones to market, Apple, with no history in the business, charged in with the iPhone and in a year snapped up a market share equal to what Motorola had taken two decades to achieve.

This growing structural weakness was increasingly apparent to outsiders, but seemingly invisible to company management. In fact, after our first book was published, I was asked to give a speech at the company about the impending shift from a supply-driven to a demand-driven economy. And I did just that, to a large group of Motorola senior managers and engineers, noting that an "innovation for its own sake" mental model, like that found at Motorola, would be increasingly obsolete in this new economic reality.[13]

We had no sooner finished these remarks when, to our surprise, Motorola's chief strategy officer jumped on the stage and announced to the assembled throng that no matter what we had just said, we were still in a supply economy . . . and that Motorola's "50,000 warring bands of engineers" philosophy would still prevail.

It was, as you might imagine, a very strange experience having your message being publicly contradicted by your hosts. Nevertheless, we couldn't let the opportunity pass—and soon the two of us on stage found ourselves in a debate. The topic was whether one could create demand where none existed—or if a company should understand existing demand and then create supply to capture a larger percentage of that demand.

Innovators argue that if you can invent a great product or service, demand will spontaneously form around it. Conversely, marketers argue that there is no such thing as a completely new product or service—rather, that the success of these new inventions is precisely due to the fact that they tap into existing pools of unfulfilled demand. It is a very old debate, and one that we believe has now been decided: in a demand-driven economy characterized by both declining (or flattened) demand and oversupply, *no* company can risk its long-term survival on a business strategy that calls for continual, untethered innovation that is not disciplined by an understanding of the available and emerging pools of demand for that innovation.

And what of Motorola and its 50,000 warring bands of engineers? The history of the company in the twenty-first century, with its long parade of missed market opportunities, late follow-up products, 10,000 layoffs, and an endless parade of spinoffs, has not been a pretty one. As Chicagoans, it's been painful for us to watch as the pride of Illinois technology has wandered around, seemingly lost, over the last decade, as its competitors have passed it by.

But it is interesting to note that in late 2008, after watching smart phone competitors Apple, Nokia, Samsung, and even RIM [Black-Berry] leave it in the technological dust, Motorola embarked on a single-minded initiative to regain its leadership in the cell phone business. It set up a skunkworks operation, hired 300 top people to staff it, and invested $50 million in it—all with the goal of emerging in a year's time with a new family of smart phones that would hold their own with any other such device on the market. In other words, Motorola decided to work backward for once, building for one giant market that already existed (the Apple iPhone) and for another that was about to emerge (the new smart phones built around the Google Android platform).

At the Consumer Electronics Show in early January 2010, Motorola introduced a new smart phone line that was the result of the previous year's initiative.[14] The Motorola Backflip featured a flip-open keyboard (like the BlackBerry) with a highly interactive user interface called "MotoBlur" (like the iPhone). Not only did the Backflip earn glowing reviews in the trade media but it was even named a "best product" at the show.

After more than eighty years, Motorola's "warring bands of engineers" were finally learning to build to the market—and not waiting for the market to come to them.

HERSHEY'S UNWRAPPED

We'll finish the chapter with a look at how one of the world's most famous candy companies, Hershey's, found—or more accurately *rediscovered*—a strong mental model, and used it to not only realign the company with a new thesis for winning, but also to reacquaint itself with the core beliefs that had first made it a success.

In 2007, we began working with the legendary Hershey Company. Hershey's was the number one confectionery company in the United States, but it was also losing share to its competitors, notably Mars. "It was an interesting time at Hershey," recalled J. P. Bilbrey, president of Hershey's North America. "After years of growth and success, we had hit a period of slowing growth. Senior management needed to bring clarity to how we were going to compete and win. We needed to create an inflection point as our results weren't as good as we would have liked them to be."[15] CEO Dave West formed a senior management team to address the challenge, said Bilbrey, "and we began to think about changing the way we thought about and ran our business."[16]

Managing iconic brands is a great privilege and Hershey's employees are passionate about the company, its brands, and its unique legacy. In addition to their responsibility to shareholders (and as shareholders) there is a strong sense of purpose when you work with the Hershey Company. The Milton Hershey Trust was formed by the founder of the company to support 2,000 low-income and needy children cared for and educated by The Milton Hershey School, founded in 1909 by Milton Hershey and his wife, Catherine.[17] There is a lot more riding on Hershey's continuing success than is the case for many companies.

On initial review, it was hard to see what was wrong with the Hershey Company. The $5 billion company[18] still had its robust portfolio of "household name" products, including Hershey's, Reese's, Kisses, Kit Kat, Twizzlers, and Ice Breakers—and we hadn't noticed any obvious drop-offs in chocolate consumption.

But looking deeper, it was clear that many of Hershey's recent strategic initiatives, especially a focus on pack types and product proliferation rather than on brands, had not produced the desired results. Worse, by creating a significant number of new SKUs based on pack types and flavor extensions, Hershey's approach was beginning to run counter to the stated desire of many retail customers to simplify the shelf by reducing product complexity.

Said Bilbrey, "While we had great brands, we had largely operated in a push mode."[19]

Soon three additional issues emerged, all beyond Hershey's control, that made the outlook for the company even more challenging.

- First, retailers were consolidating and the dynamics for growth were changing. The days of a highly fragmented retail network were long gone—a more sophisticated environment has emerged across large retailers and channels with a focus on growing categories and not simply "selling" product promotions. Advanced analytics and the understanding of how to win with consumers and shoppers is now an essential part of managing the business.

- Second, Hershey's key competitors were consolidating or were rumored to be in merger discussions. Two major competitors, Mars and Wrigley, had joined forces in 2008.[20] Meanwhile, the world's biggest chocolate company, Cadbury, was rumored to be an acquisition target—a rumor that proved true when Cadbury was acquired by Kraft in 2010.[21]

- Finally, the "great recession" that began in mid-2008 did not bode well for the industry, its retailers, or its consumers.

But there were also a number of problems that were within Hershey's control. For one thing, there was not strong alignment within the company on the "go to market" strategy. This lack of alignment led directly to the explosion of SKUs, notably a wide variety of pack types and flavor proliferations of their classic brands that Hershey's was pushing into the market.

Making this problem worse for Hershey's was the fact that, with its supply-driven approach, actual consumer demand for such products was not properly assessed. Retail partners can, of course, be an excellent source of new ideas because they are so close to local demand—but that doesn't mean these ideas should replace a disciplined innovation process (such as the one we mapped out in Chapter 5).

Without an underlying demand-driven framework at Hershey's to guide decisions, just one brand, such as Kisses, could suddenly have dozens of SKUs featuring different types of chocolate (milk chocolate, dark chocolate, white chocolate, or combinations), different fillings (caramel, peanut butter, truffle, plain), different flavors (orange, mint, cherry), with or without nuts. Adding to the complexity, each of these types of Kisses could come in a wide array of pack types, including different foil wrappers, different packages (bags, boxes), and different sizes (half-pound, ten ounces, one pound).

Needless to say, without a solid grounding in consumer demand, many of these products were not sustainable and did not perform well. Hershey's typically had to offer special promotions and deep discounts (push vs. pull) to drive sales. In the larger view, what that meant was that Hershey's had added significant cost and complexity to its supply chain to create tailored products, only to have those products fail to earn the price premium they were supposed to command. In fact, the opposite was happening. Not only did this create inefficiency within the supply chain; Hershey's was not leveraging their brand equities or meeting their core consumers' needs effectively.

Tough times. But in its more than a century of existence, Hershey's had built great brands that had survived the test of time, and the company had deep reservoirs of strength and commitment. As Bilbrey later recalled, "In retrospect, all of these issues converged at the perfect time for Hershey's, because it gave us the courage to act. We needed to go from a supply-driven approach to a demand-driven, consumer-focused one. Our existing push model was simply not sustainable. We needed to move from push to pull. Of course, that's easy to say, but much harder to do."[22]

In adversity lies opportunity—and the disappointing results and the challenging environment Hershey's faced made a strong case for a new vision at the company, one that was built on brands, consumer and shopper insights, and aligned with demand to create consumer-based pull, rather than simply pushing new products and packages into the market. Before anything else, Hershey's task was to build its new thesis for winning.

POOLS OF CHOCOLATE

We began by building for Hershey's a fact base, starting with a demand landscape for confectionery, and then understanding the demand profit pools within them. One stunning result of this groundwork was that we identified a new demand profit pool—"Engaged Exploring Munchers"—that would prove to be critical to the entire category, and to Hershey's in particular.

Just as important, once the full demand landscape was developed, it gave the entire Hershey's team for the first time a shared understanding of the total potential opportunity for the company and how to win more of it. The demand landscape made clear that the $5 billion company could access another $2 to $4 billion in profitable opportunities across the confectionery landscape in the United States.[23]

This new demand landscape was the foundation for the development of the new thesis for winning for Hershey's. It showed how and why Hershey's would win and the role each part of the organization would play in achieving that success.

It was now clear to everyone that Hershey's would win not by pushing more and different supply into the market and by focusing on pack types as it had in the past. The path forward was to develop new and deeper insights into demand, starting with the demand landscape, and to leverage and build their powerful, iconic brands. After all, while pack types and flavors could be copied by competitors, Hershey's proprietary brands could not.

Recalled J. P. Bilbrey, "When you bring the demand landscape together it allows you to understand how to compete, where there is white space, and where you are investing too much when there is little upside to be gained. We then began a process of building a single mental model across our organization to show everyone in the organization how it works and how they fit in. The business case for our mental model was very clear and compelling. The first managers to apply the new approach to their businesses saw the results and became zealots who helped others internally adopt it. We were very decisive in creating one way forward."[24]

He added, "An important part of making the mental model work was that every member of the Hershey's executive team, our leadership group, was involved in all phases of the work. Once we made the commitment to a demand business model, we were 'all in.' By creating a sense of participation across our entire leadership team, we were also creating missionaries who would go back to their own respective functional organizations and talk about the changes that were taking place on how we would run Hershey as a company."[25]

"Because of the mental model approach, we have achieved a level of collaboration within Hershey that has clarity, is aligned, and is powerful."[26]

At the same time, Hershey's also began sharing this new demand model—what it entitled "Insight Driven Performance," with its retail partners. As Bilbrey recalled, "They got it immediately. It's so intuitive that a collaborative approach is better for all parties. The idea of collaboration is important, but where everybody gets enthusiastic is when they understand that we're converting both the retailer's data and Hershey's into a single *operating system*. That's when the lights really go on. We used to talk about one activity or promotion at a time—now that we've got an operating system, each of our activities is just another app. It's easy to understand and it's easy to see the advantages."[27]

The results of Hershey's transition to a demand-driven business model have been beyond expectations. As Hershey's CEO Dave West referenced at the February 2010 meeting of the Consumer Analysts Group of New York (CAGNY), Hershey's generated record cash flows in 2009 of $1.066 billion, more than double its 2008 cash flow and 34 percent higher than the company's previous record cash flow of $797 million in 2004.[28]

The new mental model has driven alignment around how to best serve profitable demand with Hershey's unique brands. At the same time, this focus has greatly reduced complexity and cost. All of which has led to the record cash flows.

Standing at the podium that day, West told the assembled analysts that the transformation Hershey's had just gone through constituted a "fundamental regrounding in the consumer."[29] Hershey's, West said, now knew:

- *Who its consumers are*—their demographics and motivations
- *Why they buy*—their demand by profit pool and the need states they experience
- *What they buy*—a detailed understanding of the brands, packs, tastes, and textures customers most prefer
- *Where and how they buy*—shopper missions and channel preferences
- *When they consume*—the key usage occasions for confectionery.

J. P. Bilbrey summed up Hershey's renewal: "The financial implications of all of this have been really profound. Our new approach has lowered inventories, reduced SKUs, reduced complexity, created tremendous efficiencies, and generated greater cash flow. I've never seen a jump in performance like this before, so I'm going to frame this KPI report!"[30]

It was all sweet news for Hershey's. And this was just the beginning. As we'll see in the next chapter, Hershey's new mental model also set the stage for putting a competitively advantaged demand chain in place.

EIGHT

THE DEMAND CHAIN

*Collaborative Networks Power
a Profit Search Engine*

Today, perhaps more than in any time in the past eighty years, manufacturers, retailers, and media companies are all finding themselves under assault, not just by a deep global recession but by a seemingly inexplicable loss in effectiveness of some of their most important and proven business tools and strategies. These companies watch helplessly as their consumers, now networked, get smarter—and realize, to their dismay, that they aren't keeping up. The game keeps changing and the rules are evolving quickly. Clearly there's universal demand by business leaders for a new solution.

This period of economic complexity and turmoil will be a historic opportunity for some companies to gain enormous market share and profit share by participating in a new collaborative business model. This model includes a new level of collaboration and coordination between manufacturers, retailers, and media companies that goes beyond traditional data-sharing efforts and approaches such as category management.

This certainty of winning is driven by a truly proprietary understanding of what consumers demand and which of these consumers offer the greatest profitability. With these in hand, a network is formed between manufacturers, retailers, and media companies to capture the largest share of profitable demand. The commitment to this network allows all of the participants to grow at faster rates and to higher levels than would be possible without the collaboration of the network. This new model is the demand chain. It stands as the counterpoint to the traditional supply chain, its information flowing in the opposite direction, with results driving capabilities rather than the other way around.

For manufacturers it means aligning their differentiated brands and products so that they capture the highest share of the most profitable demand.

For retailers it means organizing and merchandising their stores so that they better meet the demand of the people who shop in their stores versus those of their competitors.

And for media companies it means that on the horizon there is a new level of precision that will enable them to reach the specific consumers both the manufacturers and retailers most want to communicate with and motivate.

In the collaborative environment of the demand chain, where information is shared and plans are coordinated, everyone becomes more efficient in what they make, how and where they distribute their products, and how they use their marketing and media budgets to motivate consumers and stimulate purchase behavior.

THE EUREKA MOMENT

More than 70 percent of the U.S. economy is driven by consumer spending.[1] This spending goes to businesses as diverse as food and apparel companies, over-the-counter drugs, and flat screen TVs. What they have in common is that there are three primary participants in most consumer-driven categories: the *manufacturers* who create the products, the *retailers* who comprise the vast majority of the distribution system, whether online or off line, and finally, the *media companies* whose role is to communicate with and motivate consumers on behalf of both manufacturers and retailers.

Manufacturers have focused on consumers for decades. Meanwhile, retailers attempted to attract an increasing share of shoppers. And at the same time, media companies were attempting to attract viewers and listeners. Only recently has it become clear that while each of the three was looking through its own lens, they were all in the end trying to attract the very same person.

It was this realization that the same consumer was being pursued by manufacturers, retailers, and media companies that led to the creation of the demand chain. Since everyone was pursuing the same person, what if they could share all of their data in a new network of collaboration? That would enable each of the three to know more, to act cooperatively, and to have an enormous competitive advantage over competitors who were continuing to follow their traditional isolated course.

Best of all, such a collaboration could also produce the network effects of Metcalfe's law—that is, this new lens would actually *magnify* the results as efficiencies, innovation, and new parts of the network came onstream—and would not only be beneficial for current and future users of the network, but also be good for the consumers the demand chain was designed to serve. Now, for the first time, manufacturers, retailers, and media companies would have an upward pathway out of their current predicament.

A CHAIN OF EVENTS

The demand chain is emerging at a time when manufacturers, retailers, and media companies are all under significant pressure. While some of this difficulty is driven by the recession, many of the issues are structural and will remain in place even as the economy improves. To recapitulate:

Manufacturers are facing flattening or contracting demand. With unemployment stubbornly high, and millions of people underemployed, there is less disposable income to spend on products and services. In addition, retailers across the world are promoting their improved private-label products while reducing the shelf space given to branded products. The difficult economy also has shifted spending away from premium products to more lower-cost and value-priced brands. Finally, the same supply-chain efficiencies manufacturers have used for decades add to the growing issue of oversupply facing most industries.

Retailers were carried along by the overexpansion and profligate borrowing of the past several years. Many thought it a smart strategy to keep up with the burgeoning demand they were seeing by opening new, larger stores. Surely, they told themselves, the customers who were loading their credit cards with new levels of debt, as well as the customers who came to their stores flush with spending power after taking out home equity loans, would all continue to spend at the same breathless pace as they had in the past several years. As we now know, that feverish spending came to an abrupt halt . . . and now many retailers are left with too many retail stores, and "too many doors."

This sudden threat to manufacturers and retailers spread quickly to *media companies*, whose primary advertisers were precisely those manufacturers and retailers. Media companies, which had also experienced years of continued prosperity, found themselves facing deeply cut advertising and marketing budgets and unsold minutes of radio and TV. Even more deeply affected were the magazines and newspapers, whose business was moving to the new media of the Internet at lighting speed.

The architecture and processes of the demand chain offer these threatened manufacturers, retailers, and media companies a new competitive advantage—one that is certain to help those who implement it overcome some of the competitive (as well as economic) issues they face today.

Here is our definition of the demand chain:

A demand chain is a collaborative network composed of manufacturer, retailers, and media companies that enable each participant to better understand—and more completely and precisely fulfill—customer demand.

THE MANUFACTURER'S PERSPECTIVE

Let us describe the demand chain in detail from the standpoint of a manufacturer that creates the linkages to retailers and to media companies. (Demand chains can, as we said, originate with retailers—but for purposes of simplicity we'll begin with a manufacturer example.)

At the top of the triad is the manufacturer. As described in earlier chapters, by using the tools of what we call "demand strategy"—macroeconomic analysis, demand profit pools, and other analytic tools such as need states—this manufacturer can build a proprietary understanding of current, latent, and emerging demand in the categories of products it manufactures.

The Demand Chain

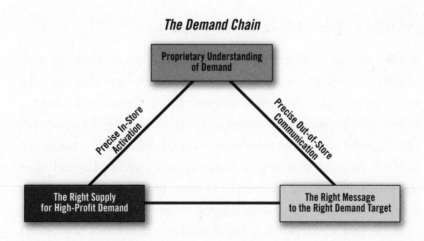

Critical to the understanding of this triad are demand profit pools and the profit each pool represents for the manufacturer. The profitability of each pool determines the allocation of resources that are then deployed through both retailers and the media in the rest of the demand chain.

In a traditional business model, this proprietary understanding of demand would remain with the manufacturer, whose executives in marketing, sales, marketing research, and production, as well as the CEO and the senior executives reporting to him or her, would convert that understanding into strategies, tactics, and communications for each line of business and for each brand. These strategies and plans would then form the basis for future selling strategies and communications.

In the demand chain, all that we've just described remains in place. What changes is that the intellectual capital created by the demand strategy is now shared with all other participants in the demand chain, both retailers and media, who in return share their own data with the manufacturer. At this point of collaboration and sharing, the demand chain takes form and gains its true competitive advantage.

MANUFACTURERS *PLUS* RETAILERS

It has long been understood that for major retailers, different stores in different neighborhoods attract different customers who carry different types of demand. For a supermarket, for instance, a suburban store would probably cater to families with children, while a store in a city might serve an older population without children at home, or perhaps a large group of young professionals and students. Depending on the neighborhood and the people who live in that neighborhood, the demand to be served by a store is going to vary dramatically.

In the best scenario, the types of products, the brands of products, and their price points should differ by store. Even package sizes should vary widely, with a home with two parents and three children offered large packages, and single or two-person households presented with smaller packages. Finally, the needs of shoppers who are far more focused on price or others who are more focused on quality (such as in fresh foods and perishables) would also be met.

In other words, different stores should serve distinctly different types of demand. Imagine if the manufacturer and retailer were to collaborate and share information so that for each individual store, the supply on the shelves were directly aligned with the demand of the people who shop in that store. While no more than a dream just a short time ago, the demand chain creates the opportunity to make this a reality—and in doing so, to fully realize Adam Smith's[2] core economic premise. If you align supply to meet the demand you want to serve, you more fully satisfy your customer, you have the opportunity to create pricing power, and you create higher levels of loyalty among your customers.

Today, we are building demand chains between manufacturers and retailers with a high level of precision. For example, for a beverage company that sells its thirty brands in thousands of stores across several different channels, we have made it possible for each store to:

- Determine which brands should be in each store
- Determine the assortment or the amount of each brand in each store
- Determine which package types are preferred by the people who shop in that store
- Create the promotional or point-of-sale materials that are unique to the demand of the people shopping in that store
- Establish a pricing strategy that creates the highest level of sales and the highest level of profit can be determined for each store

The demand chain is expressed through individual stores, and that would seem to make it very complex. What makes it entirely practical is that retailers of all kinds are already segmenting or classifying their stores into five or six different clusters. Therefore, though thousands of stores are being served by our beverage company, all are assigned to one of the five or six clusters, each serving similar types of consumer demand. And so, while the customization of brand, assortment, pack type, etc., varies store by store, each of these stores is in turn part of a larger group that can be efficiently encompassed by the demand chain.

How is it done? It begins with a collection of analytics, databases, and purchase-behavior statistics that are brought together and put through a series of steps. At each step there are statisticians, econometricians, and a whole team of hard-working people who combine all of the data into a practical, usable, and profit-building tool that links manufacturers to retailers and retailers back to manufacturers.

The demand chain is a very simple concept, but does require a number of steps to bring it fully alive. Perhaps the best way to understand how the demand chain works between manufacturers and retailers can be seen in the diagram on page 199.

One of the early adopters of the demand chain was the Hershey Company. In a company meeting, President J. P. Bilbrey and Vice President of Sales Dan Vukovich simplified the idea with a very contemporary, analogy. The demand chain, they said, is like the Apple iPhone: at its heart is an operating system formed by the shared data of manufacturer, retailer, and media companies to the profitable benefit of all. Meanwhile, everything that takes place between the manufacturer and the retailer—and all of the activities in the retail store—are simply a series of applications.[3] In just a few seconds, the power and ultimate simplicity of the demand chain was expressed through the most everyday example imaginable. It couldn't get any better than that.

That raises two interesting questions: if the demand chain is so useful, how many such chains will there be? One might well have asked the same question about the supply chain thirty years ago. We believe there will be hundreds, perhaps thousands, of demand chains. There are hundreds of product categories, each one having the potential to form a unique demand chain with each of the hundreds of retailers who sell their product. In turn, the demand chains will be linked to media companies. This is a classic case of first-mover advantage.

Second, who should initiate a demand chain—the manufacturer or the retailer? The fact is that it doesn't matter who starts a demand chain, only whether or not you are participating with your most valued manufacturers and retailers.

MATCHING CHAINS

We are halfway there. Now we have to complete the other side of the triad. We now know we can architect each store for maximum profits; the next step is to look outward to the media.

In developing this other side of the triad, we turned to our colleagues at Nielsen. Their media measurement services are the world's standard. Was it possible, we asked, to isolate the particular media that each demand profit pool used the most? As it happened, media research companies (including our own Nielsen Media Group) were already asking themselves a similar question: can we help advertisers identify the media most favored by different segments of consumers?

The result turned out to be good news, especially for national television and Internet sites and blogs. The ability to identify the right media for the right consumer *can* become more precise, and work has been ongoing for the past two years. Nielsen, for example, already had a large group of people working on the complex topic of matching different demand profit pools to their favorite national TV programs and to their favored Internet sites and blogs.

Progress is being made. Nielsen currently has a product it calls Fusion,[4] which can link manufacturers and retailers more precisely to their high-profit consumers through national TV and the Internet. The only requirement is that all parties work together to establish the matching characteristics of the consumer that is shared by the manufacturer, the retailer, and the media company. And by 2012, there likely will be an architecture in place through which Nielsen will be able to tell an advertiser which national TV shows, which Internet sites, and which blogs their targeted high-profit consumers frequent most often.

This analysis will use demographics, but will go further. New technology, new Internet tools, the networking relationship, and most important, the shared data of the demand chain will enable media companies to match high-profit consumers to their favorite national TV programs and to their most-visited Internet sites and blogs. It will be another important link in the demand chain—and a vital step toward the precision of finding and appealing to the consumers a company most covets in order to grow share of market, revenues, and profits.

This will not only increase return on advertising dollars for the advertiser; it will also enable media companies for the first time to ensure their clients that their advertising and promotional budgets will actually reach intended consumer targets in the manner, and with the power, they've always dreamed of.

What we at Nielsen and Cambridge bring to this revolution is the language and tools that will help companies realize the full potential of the demand chain. We have been pioneers in this field, but soon there will be an explosion of tools and techniques as more and more corporate marketing departments and growth-strategy consulting firms begin applying their intellectual capital to the challenge of demand.

Implicit in our definition is that the demand chain is about building a significantly more intimate and effective connection between consumers, manufacturers, retailers, and media companies. This connection has one goal: to determine in which stores the consumers who carry the most valuable demand can be found—and how they can best be reached through the national TV and the Internet sites and blogs they most frequently visit.

When the demand chain is in place, the end result is optimized profitability for each player in that chain:

- The manufacturer's profits will be driven by having the right products, the right pack types, the right assortment, and the right point-of-sale materials that are aligned to the demand of the consumers who shop in that store.

- The profits of retailers will increase when the merchandise in their stores aligns closely with the demand of their most valued shoppers.

- For media companies, the profit search engine is engaged when they are able to target more precisely the most valuable consumers for both the retailer and the manufacturer. This is accomplished by building on demographics and using identifying characteristics from both the manufacturer and the retailer that will enable greater precision in finding the highest-valued targets. With improved delivery of the high-value consumer and shopper, the value of the media inventory will increase.

HERSHEY'S, REVISITED

Let's now return to the Hershey's case study, in light of what we've just learned about the demand chain.

Despite the enormous success of its new demand-driven mental model—and the record cash flows it helped generate—Hershey's management team wanted to do more to ensure that this was not a short-term victory but a long-term strategy. And the team knew exactly which issue the company needed to address to consolidate its gains: *scale.*

Historically, being America's largest confectioner, Hershey's didn't have to worry much about scale—that was its competitors' problem. But with the recent mergers of Mars and Wrigley, as well as Cadbury and Kraft—both creating larger multicategory competitors—

Hershey's suddenly found itself, for almost the first time in its history, at a size disadvantage.

Giant Kraft, the second-largest food and beverage company in the world, could take advantage of its existing importance to retailers across multiple categories in stores; in other words, Hershey's was no longer competing against the cross-linkages of Cadbury chocolate bars, Certs, and Chiclets (among others), but now against hundreds of products from Oscar Mayer hot dogs to Oreos to Velveeta.

And if Kraft owned most of the shelves in the typical supermarket, Mars/Wrigley played a significant role in the check-out aisles in those same supermarkets with a broad portfolio of chocolates, gums, hard candies, and mints, all designed to attract the attention of the customer while he or she waited for the cashier. Hershey's, by comparison, was focused on only one category—and while it was the biggest name in that category, the company had to think about "scale" differently with these newly merged competitors.

Hershey's president, J. P. Bilbrey, and his team realized that if they were going to stay in the game they were going to have to change the rules, to take advantage of Hershey's considerable intellectual capital to create fundamentally new types of scale advantage. The idea would be to create that advantage from big ideas and big insights, rather than from big companies and big categories.

As we joined in these conversations, it struck us that with the demand profit pools identified and a new mental model in place, it might be possible for Hershey's to build one of the first true demand chains—and in the process harness those big ideas to gain a market advantage. It might even be possible, we realized, to use that demand chain to counterbalance any advantages in size Hershey's competitors might now have.

DAVID AND GOLIATH

For Hershey's, the powerful promise of the demand chain was to optimize results for itself and its retail partners. It would do so by creating a demand profile for each store that would in turn allow Hershey's and its retail partners to make and sell:

- The right brands
- The right pack types
- The right retail/shopper programs
- The right retail execution
- The right marketing and media

This can only be accomplished if all of the players in the chain agree on a common view of demand that brings together the manufacturer's view of the market and the consumers within it with the retailer's view of the marketplace, their shoppers, and the "trip missions" that drive shopping. These trip missions can include anything from the major weekly trip to the grocery store, to a fill-in trip for items like milk that are consumed quickly, to a special occasion mission for cake and ice cream to celebrate a birthday, to a focused trip for cold medicine at the drugstore.

As J. P. Bilbrey described it, "Retailers have a ton of data about shoppers and trip missions. Our data is more consumer-oriented—*why* they buy rather than *where* they buy. Despite the fact that these two bodies of data are complementary, no one before had ever really figured out how to bring all of this together efficiently. Everyone just had half of the picture—when we all really needed the whole picture."[5]

It took Hershey's several months to complete this integration. The resulting integrated operating system for retailers—the Insight Driven Performance (IDP) program described earlier—has proven to be one of the most important structural innovations in the company's recent history.

Today, IDP is being deployed in a growing list of retail programs to optimize sales and profits for both Hershey's and the individual retailers. Its elements include:

- Creating demand profiles for each retailer;

- Clustering similar retailers to tailor the right brands;

- Creating the best assortment of brands, SKUs, and pack types for each unique retailer cluster; and

- Designing sales programs, merchandising, and marketing to yield optimum results for the specific store profiles in each cluster.

And the list continues to grow.

Says Bilbrey: "Our customers—that is, retailers—have really responded to IDP because they get it immediately. For them, it is now no longer 'me versus you,' but the synergy of driving toward greater efficiencies and greater profits *together*. For the first time, the process is collaborative. And it is all coming together in a way that makes size much less important, because we have developed *intellectual scale*."[6]

In the David-and-Goliath business that the confectionery business has become, one-time giant Hershey's has discovered that there is more than one way to win big.

NINE

SUPPLY, MEET DEMAND

The Partnership of Supply and Demand

In our work, we frequently see examples of companies that are doing everything right by the old rules but now find themselves in a desperate search for increasingly elusive growth.

In one case, the CEO of a large consumer goods manufacturer lamented that the results of his company's focus on supply chain reengineering had been successful—but failed to deliver any insight into its customers. As he told us, in what could be the epitaph for many companies in the years to come: "For the past few years we have been focused on reengineering our entire supply chain. As a result, we now get the wrong products to the wrong customers at the wrong stores faster and cheaper than anyone else."[1]

To be sure, the supply chain has created competitive advantage for those companies that use Six Sigma and other approaches to ensure lower costs, faster cycle time, and higher quality supply. The need to get your supply chain right will not change in the future.

What *will* change is the way you will leverage that supply chain in order to win. Competitive advantage is no longer going to accrue solely from developing a supply chain that is faster and lower cost, and ensures higher quality—and, as we've tried to show you, you must adapt to that change.

In the years to come, the real power of the supply chain will have less to do with the micromanagement of details regarding cost and performance, or with one's comparative advantage relative to competitors' supply chains. Instead, the true measure of power for one's supply chain will now lie in its ability to more precisely target and serve the right demand at the right time at the right place in the right package and in the right environment. Supply chain advantage will now be driven by how closely it is guided by, and responsive to, the demand chain as it enables the supply chain to deliver the right product to the right place at the right time.

Simply put: *Your supply chain can no longer be optimized without a complimentary, and equally optimized, demand chain.*

Unfortunately, very few companies today exhibit this balance.

As the CEO quoted at the beginning of this chapter makes perfectly clear, one potential danger of having supply-chain improvement become a goal in and of itself is that this goal can become disconnected from its real purpose: fulfilling customer demand. In the new connection, the demand chain's fundamental role is to architect what *should be* on each retailer's shelf. The difference in revenues and profits from using the supply chain to replace what *is now* on the shelf with what *should be there* will create the margin of victory for the companies who adopt the new business model.

Going forward, winning supply chains will precisely align demand and supply in ways that have never before been possible. New technologies, combined with the intellectual capital of demand profit pools, will afford companies the ability to align the right supply to precisely the right demand—thus enabling growth in the only way possible in flat markets: taking volume, share, and profits from your competitors.

One important implication of this is that managers will need to focus much greater attention on:

1. *Identifying* the target, highly attractive demand profit pools of customers; and

2. *Determining* how the supply chain can best respond to, and satisfy, this precise group of consumers.

The strategy of having a demand-led supply chain goes beyond organizational alignment; it is in fact a structural change with enormous implications for organizational efficiency and continual profitability. While the most obvious benefit is to ensure that what should be on the shelf is what you actually have in place, the implications go far beyond improving the alignment of demand and supply at the retailer's shelf. There are four key benefits.

1. Start Better

One of the first benefits of this partnership is the demand chain's ability to get the right product to the right retail outlet at the right time. This essentially converts the supply chain from its current task of replacing what is on the shelf today with more of the same to that of determining what *should be* on the shelf.

This is more important than most companies realize: if your starting assumptions are flawed, the supply chain will not correct for that fact. If you are selling 100 cans of regular dog food per week, the supply chain is going to replenish those 100 cans of regular dog food each week, while adjusting for promotions that could have an impact on weekly sales. What the supply chain will never tell you is that you could significantly increase profits by aligning with the demand that store can support for higher-margin premium dog foods and more healthful dog foods aimed at the Pampering Parents and Performance Fuelers demand profit pools. You are leaving profits on the table—and you will never know it.

By comparison, incorporating insights from the demand chain

completes the evolution of the supply chain from push to pull—and ultimately, to a whole new level of precision based on demand rather than process. That is, most supply chains start by pushing products into distribution channels based on forecasts. These forecasts are built on certain assumptions that, if false or inaccurate, can lead to overproduction, out-of-stocks, obsolescence, and customer dissatisfaction.

Given these problems with the push system and the forecasts it is built on, many companies have begun to reengineer their supply chains to transition to a pull system. In a pull system, raw materials, work in process, and finished goods are pulled through the supply chain based on predefined inventory levels at each step, rather than pushed through the supply chain based on forecasted needs. While the pull system has created tremendous efficiencies and improved supply chain performance overall, it is important not to confuse knowledge of actual purchases with truly understanding demand.

The level of precision created by the demand chain is the next generation for optimizing the supply chain. Not only will you start out with what should be on the shelf; you will have a combination of mechanisms that consistently evolve with consumer demand, and be far ahead of your competitors in capturing emerging demand.

The "sense and response" mechanisms in current supply chains will be greatly enhanced with the input of the demand chain. Forecasting will be improved and trends will not only improve the supply chain but will also create hypotheses for innovation. Ultimately, while the supply chain *takes cost out* of the system, the demand chain *puts profits back into* the system.

2. Communicate Better

One of the great joys of being in retail is the real-time ability to execute ideas and make changes based on market conditions and opportunities. While this is a great benefit for the retailer, it can create significant problems for the manufacturer's supply chain in forecasting, production, and accuracy. Being reliant on inputs, the supply chain is suboptimized when it's unable to respond to changes made by retailers. This is particularly true for the seasonal products that are so important in so many consumer categories.

In the shared network of the demand chain, the communication between retailers and manufacturers improves greatly. The improved communication is the result of shared data, shared inputs, and shared outputs. The result enables better coordination and provides consistent opportunities for high-level supply chain performance.

3. Align Better

This balanced approach also drives much greater internal alignment and communication. As the benefits of the partnership between the demand chain and supply chain become apparent, it fosters further collaboration and helps resolve the potential tension between identifying and responding to demand opportunities and the desire to maintain the discipline of the supply chain.

As we described in Chapter 7, the aligned corporation is the winning corporation. The convergence of the demand chain and the supply chain will provide a shared lens through which marketing, sales, manufacturing, distribution, and supply chain management can view both the demand and the supply of their business. The result is better communication, better understanding, and improved performance for both the demand chain and the supply chain, and the people who manage and are responsible for both chains.

4. Structure Better

Over time, this partnership leads to improvements in the overall structure of the supply chain and its ability to serve profitable demand.

Fully informed by an understanding of demand on a store-by-store, local market, regional, and national level, the flexibility, adaptability, and responsiveness of the supply chain can be improved. Managers can reconfigure where manufacturing is located, how to coordinate production capacity, where and how to locate warehouses, and how best to distribute products most efficiently—all informed by the understanding of demand that flows from the demand chain.

As one contemplates flat or contracting demand, finding large veins of high-margin profitability becomes extremely elusive. We arrived at this when we were working with a client on the financial benefits that would be realized when the demand chain would actually lead the supply chain. While we were optimistic, what started as a theory has turned into the promise of revenue and profit opportunities that should equal or perhaps even exceed those achieved by the supply chain alone.

The financial benefits of aligning the demand chain to the supply chain include both revenue growth, cost savings, and/or improved asset utilization:

Revenue growth

- Reduced out-of-stocks and lost sales for both retailer and manufacturer

- Capture of white-space opportunity at a local market level (latent and emerging demand)

- Higher velocity/greater buy rate due to better performing products and less obsolescence

- More space for new product introductions—facings become available due to greater shelf productivity

- Greater price realization due to reduced mark-downs, especially for seasonal products

Cost savings or improved asset utilization

- Lower inventory carrying costs and working capital

- Reduced product obsolescence or raw material scrappage for seasonal products

- Reduced need for high-cost production during peak periods due to poor forecasts (e.g., less co-packing)

- Higher plant efficiencies/lower conversion costs due to a more accurate production plan

- More efficient truck routing or reduced midday reloads due to high out-of-stocks or wrong truck loading

- Avoidance of capital expenditures to create excess capacity or flexible production to compensate for poor demand forecast

It should be noted that these cost savings are in addition to those realized in sales and marketing, such as:

- More efficient direct marketing expenditure (DME)

- More efficient trade promotion/trade spend

- More efficient media spend

One company that is realizing the benefits of a strong partnership between the demand chain and the supply chain is the Spanish apparel manufacturer and retailer Zara. In Zara's case, these benefits have been achieved through vertical integration as they both manufacture and sell apparel. Zara is one of the most successful apparel companies in the world and has experienced explosive growth precisely because it has a deep understanding of customer demand and responds quickly to the changing fashions sought by its trendy shoppers. The fast-moving fashions offered by Zara encourage customers to stop in frequently to see what is new and to buy immediately, before the product line changes. While Zara has achieved its success through vertical integration, the collaborative network of the demand chain will allow any company to realize similar benefits through virtual integration.

THE IMPORTANCE OF EARLY WARNING AND EMERGING OPPORTUNITY

In a world that moves at the speed of the Internet and provides virtually perfect choice, one of the most important skills of demand-driven companies will be the ability to understand patterns of behavior faster than their competitors. Pessimists would call this an "early warning system." We prefer to call it an "early opportunity system."

Companies that win will have a robust early opportunity system embedded in their demand chain that alerts them to shifts in demand—and is then tightly integrated with a supply chain that has the flexibility to respond quickly to these shifts with the right offerings.

New tools and technologies are emerging for just this sort of early warning/opportunity system, or at least aspects of it. One of the most promising takes advantage of the vast world of "consumer generated media" such as MySpace, Facebook, and YouTube, not to mention the millions of blogs and bulletin boards, many of them dedicated to particular products, companies, and services.

Today, surprisingly few companies—especially those in nonconsumer goods—have any real understanding of the blogosphere, social networks, or other online networks. In particular, few have any idea what is being said on those sites, chat rooms, and tweets about their company, much less the impact of those comments. At best, a growing number of CEOs and other managers have put into place systems that enable them to review a page or two of blog entries each morning to get a sense of what consumers are saying. But that isn't enough; it is merely raw data when sophisticated analysis and insight are needed.

We will say it again: the modern company exists inside of a much larger community of customers, suppliers, distributors, retailers, and other stakeholders. And the company's fate is very much tied to the health and happiness of this larger "family"—if one part of this community begins to fail or become disenchanted, every part will be affected. That's why you need to identify problem areas (as well as successes, new ideas, and best practices) as quickly as they occur and respond to them. Today, few companies have the information apparatus or the tools to accomplish that. Therefore, they don't really understand what these communities thought about their company and its offerings yesterday or think about them today—and they certainly don't understand the implications of these attitudes for tomorrow.

In winning companies, consumer-generated media becomes an important input to both the demand chain and the supply chain. It's not just listening to these communities; it is developing an ability to query and communicate with those communities in ways that provide valuable insights into how demand is shifting and what competitors are doing, and that receive advance warning about emerging new competitors.

The ability to integrate consumer-generated media with more formalized marketing research data will become an invaluable part of the demand chain. In turn, the supply chain will have an additional sense-and-respond mechanism to enable it to more precisely target the right product to the right customer at the right place.

This process has already begun. Best Buy wins by understanding its target Enthusiasts and the critical need states they experience (for example, Fun-Filled Free Time) in greater depth than the competition, and then it continually improves the ways they serve them.

Going forward, companies like Best Buy, Anheuser-Busch, and others will win because, based on their "touch" with the marketplace and verified by consumer research, they've developed an inherent sense of latent and emerging demand, and because they've now got a supply chain adaptable enough to respond to those changes. Ultimately, as we've famously seen with Apple, these companies will develop a kind of sixth sense in terms of knowing what the next big opportunity is for their highly profitable target consumers. They will be distinguished by their ability to look around the corner and see what is coming. And that will make them very tough competitors.

INTEGRATING SUPPLY AND DEMAND

In the demand-driven economy, the supply chain will respond to shifts in demand, as identified by the demand chain, as a natural act—not as an awkward, forced fit. The supply chain will configure itself around the opportunities on the horizon, and will keep evolving that way. In too many companies today, supply chains fight these types of changes. They try to divorce cost position from profit potential because the flexibility required to serve latent and emerging demand is in conflict with the long, homogeneous production runs that have traditionally driven supply chain efficiency.

That entrenched position is no longer viable. While sensing demand shifts earlier and at a deeper need state level than anyone else will become the definitive competitive advantage, lowering costs by fine tuning supply will always be of value. Consumers who want your product are your biggest demand pool—and if you can tune your supply chain to reach that pool first and satisfy their need states better, you will build a relationship with those customers that your competitors will find almost impossible to penetrate.

But to do so means constantly probing, experimenting, testing, and learning about your target demand pools and their need states. You will need to know what you're looking for. If there's a twitch in need states, or a new community forms, you will know why. Common threads appear quickly and create new opportunities—and you will have to be quick enough and attentive enough to spot them. These days, marketing needs to be at least as quick as supply.

By the same token, once a new opportunity is recognized, it has to be acted on quickly. An understanding of that opportunity, and the pressing need to act on it, has to proliferate quickly through the company. It has to be translated into a solution to bring to market. And the whole company must align to execute that solution—not least the supply chain, which must rapidly reorganize to adapt to this new demand. It is an adaptive supply chain.

It goes without saying that speed is of the essence throughout this process. Most managers equate obsolescence with physical inventory, but ideas can become obsolete, too. In fact, the shelf life of a good idea is often shorter—and much more valuable—than the shelf life of physical products. Recall from our discussion of innovation in Chapter 5 how knowledge capital or intellectual capital has become a more significant driver of the overall value of a company than its tangible assets, such as inventories. Intellectual capital is the new currency; it is what is valued most.

So how do you achieve this fast cycle response time? By being as adaptive and mutable as the markets you are dealing with. We believe that means running ten to twenty small test-and-learn experiments *all the time* rather than one or two major "put a man on the moon" initiatives. It also means responding quickly with an initial offer or prototype for target consumers and then engaging them in the process of refining it over time—rather than following the traditional model of taking months and months to perfect and then launch a "finalized" offer. The reality is that your finalized offer will need to be improved and refined almost from the moment it is launched anyhow. Take a look at Google: it typically lists its new products as beta for years[2]—a recognition that when it comes to Web tools, there is almost never a finished product, merely the latest version. The whole experience is one of continual improvement and innovation. Everybody in the organization is permanently focused on what's next.

Another example is the Apple iPhone. Its introduction at the Apple Users Meeting in early January 2007, nearly seven months before its first shipment, was as much a lure to attract developers and advice from its army of loyal Apple users as it was a formal announcement.[3] Breaking with its own history, Apple then decided not to develop applications software for the iPhone internally, but to make design tools available to developers. And three years later, there are more than 100,000 applications (more than any one company could ever develop), of which more than *one billion* copies have been downloaded by users. This universe of software, with an application for every imaginable user need state, not only proved to be the iPhone's biggest selling point but also its greatest defense against the arrival of the comparable Google Android phone two years later.

A NEW ROLE FOR LEADERSHIP

We would be remiss in this chapter if we only spoke to the opportunity that the partnership of demand chain and supply chain will provide. To achieve all that this partnership promises, leaders, including the CEO, will have to envision and then make real the benefits of this new partnership.

There is almost always a tension within a company between the tangibility and precision of the supply chain and its supply-driven mentality, and the more intangible and creative dimension of the demand side of the business. CEOs and senior managers will have to lead, encourage, and incent those responsible for bringing the supply chain and the demand chain together. But at the same time they have to manage precision to make those potential opportunities real, not just interesting hypotheses.

It would be naïve to think there isn't a natural conflict in this. The danger is having these two groups working at cross-purposes rather than aligning behind demand. It would be a nightmare for all involved to have one wildly creative part of the team constantly chasing new demand opportunities while the rest of the team wants to constantly refine and perfect existing offers. The predictable result would be entropy in the process, cycle-time increases, and in the end, nothing productive built or delivered.

Traditionally, great supply chains have improved cost, quality, and cycle time by favoring homogeneous demand. It is precisely the scale of the financial benefits and the scope of the competitive benefits that make the integration of the demand chain and the supply chain one of the highest-priority initiatives for winning in the future. As is always the case in great leaps forward, it is the skilled management team that both sees and seizes the opportunity.

None of this should be intimidating; it should be motivating. As we said early in this chapter, the partnership of the demand chain and the supply chain is likely the purest and most powerful expression of the law of supply and demand. You've spent twenty years perfecting your supply chain. Its next evolution is to be guided by an equally powerful demand chain. This is the competitive advantage and the margin of victory in the twenty-first century.

A FRESH START

Tough times make great companies.

That's the unspoken rule in almost every industry. Nobody wishes for economic downturns or major economic transformations. And few companies even prepare for them. We naturally prefer long intervals of predictable change, steady growth, and as few changes as possible to the status quo. That's because even poorly run companies can be successful during good times, and good companies can be hugely successful.

But hard times do come on a regular basis. And once or twice in everyone's career, the entire economy seems to go upside down. Then, suddenly, all of the rules have changed.

We are in one of those times. We grew very comfortable and complacent with a perpetually growing global economy that would buy everything we produced—even if only at a discount. But those days are over. It should be apparent to even the most resistant reader that what we are going through these days is not the standard quadrennial economic cycle, but something much more systemic—and that the global economy that emerges from this downturn will be quite different from the one we just left.

We have made the case, backed by extensive data, that what we are now experiencing is a kind of tectonic shift in the global economy from a marketplace based on a relative equilibrium between supply and demand to one characterized by a dangerous combination of oversupply and declining (or at best, flattening) demand. Oversupply is, ironically, the product of modern companies being *too good* at making things; declining demand, the result of a global recession, high unemployment, a shortage of credit, and everyday folks understandably saving more money for an unpredictable future.

Some of this will get better in the months and years to come. But in a larger sense, *everything* has changed. The flipping of supply and demand has been in the works now for 200 years. And though we hardly noticed, the rise of the demand-driven economy began almost a generation ago, long before our current troubles.

As they say in Silicon Valley, "During good times, everybody's a genius." Economic booms cover up a lot of weaknesses and mistakes; economic busts expose those flaws and attack them. Hard times separate the good companies and the good managers. Great economic transformations are the true character tests for corporations—and they reward those that pass this test with both competitive advantages and expanded market shares that can endure for decades.

On the other hand, those companies that are unprepared—or refuse to become prepared—for this new economic reality are already watching their profits being squeezed, experiencing a burst of new competitors that appear from around the world, and suffering from an inability to react as fast as the new challenges fly at them. For them, none of the old tricks seem to work anymore. They no longer understand their customers; their supply channels are filled to overflowing; their retailers are not only cutting back on units but entire categories; and thanks to discounting and other desperate tactics, their profit margins are getting squeezed.

Worst of all, every initiative these companies have used in the past to improve their financials—cutting prices, improving the supply chain, adding more product features—now only seem to make things *worse.* They are in a downward, vicious cycle and they have no strategy for climbing out of it.

Smart companies are feeling these same threats, but they will survive this character test. They'll do so by being adaptive and resilient. In the end they will accept the inevitability of the new economic order—and even embrace it. They will develop new strategies, find new tools, retrain their employees, and seek out and serve the right suppliers, distributors, retailers, and most of all, the right customers, to not only survive this change, but to *win.*

MONDAY MORNING

None of this will happen overnight. But you can begin right now, asking some tough questions about yourself, your company, your competitors, and your category.

Do you understand the technology driving the consumer revolution?

In my (Dave) early days at General Electric—this was in the early 1990s—my boss Jack Welch forced me to read an inch-thick manual on a new technology called "the Internet." And he didn't stop there: just to make sure that I fully incorporated the Web into my professional life, Welch then assigned a bright young person to work with me and to make sure all of my questions were answered. Jack understood that it wasn't enough to talk about new technologies and how they might influence our business; we had to *live* the technology, just as our suppliers and customers did.

This is never easy, and it only gets more difficult the older you are. But it is an absolute necessity. You need to get out of your comfort zone and participate in the ever changing, technology-driven world. The good news is that there are a lot of people out there willing to help you.

Do you know how to reach your newly organized consumer?

Over the last few years, hundreds of millions of consumers around the world have used IMs, tweets, LinkedIn networks, fandom to popular blogs, and Facebook pages to organize themselves into brand-new social, political, and economic groups. These real and virtual communities and neighborhoods are remarkably sophisticated—and increasingly difficult for outsiders to enter. Do you understand the nature of *all* of the social groups to which your customers are now engaged? Do you have a strategy for reaching them in those locations—that is, gain entry? Do you have a way to assess your customers' need states while they are in those locations?

Ultimately you and your competitors are in a race, and the winner will be the one who better satisfies the demand, in all of its forms, of your high-profit consumers. Many of the answers will be found in those new communities of your newly organized consumers . . . *if* you know where to look and can gain entry.

Have you discovered the power of demand profit pools?

It is a new way to think of organizing into segments consumers whose demand for a product or service is shared. You'll find tools that enable you to understand the profitability of each demand profit pool and how to more precisely reach and motivate consumers who create by far the most value for you and your shareholders.

Have you built a vision around rapidly changing consumers that includes their need states?

Recall that need states are the circumstances or the occasions that cause you to want something and to take action in its pursuit. Think of how Bud Light Lime understood that at outdoor occasions in the summer, consumers wanted a beer with a sweeter palate.[1] Or how it was Gatorade that invented the need state of the "hot and sweaty" occasion and built its business around proprietary insights into that need state that their competitors lacked.[2] Need states allow for greater competitive differentiation because they are directly linked to why consumers make specific purchases.

Is your organizational understanding of need states sufficiently precise that your supply chain can have the right product available to satisfy the need state the consumer brings to the purchase occasion? Consumers have growing choices, and for companies who understand need states and their importance to consumer decisions, it's like a secret weapon.

Are you committed to understanding and acting on virtual consumption?

Consumers are talking more now than ever before—and in the process, conveying enormous amounts of information about themselves: their desires, tastes, interests, dislikes, needs. They are doing so over the phone, via e-mail, tweets, Web searches, instant polls, online bulletin boards, personal Web pages, and on and on. Is your business model applying enough resources to effectively acquire that information on a timely basis?

By definition, consumers *consume*, and these days that consumption includes not just products but ideas. Products and services are no longer just things, but cultures and community. Do you understand this culture? Are you serving it? Do you know how to influence it? Do you know if there are bloggers or Web sites out there—pro or con—devoted to your products or services? Do you monitor them, and are you engaged with them?

The culture of a product today can be just as important as the product itself. Smart companies—such as Procter & Gamble with its huge Pampers Facebook family[3] and Kraft with the "eating at home" community[4]—support those communities with the understanding that their members are the companies' most important advocates. Are you a key influencer in the communities of your products and services?

Are you as committed to your demand chain as you are to your supply chain?

Building and maintaining a demand chain is a new skill, but everything you need to do so is already available. Imagine a collaborative network between manufacturers, retailers, and the media where shared information creates true alignment, true excellence, true efficiencies, and higher profits for all who participate in that network.

But nothing will happen unless you are first willing to make the same kind of commitment to your demand chain as you have made to your supply chain. More than anything, that means building an intelligence system that emphasizes latent and emerging demand as much as it does current demand. This means putting into place an apparatus capable of capturing and conveying a stream of data about these three types of demand from blogs, Web sites, bulletin-board postings, and so on, and converting your marketing research data into actionable analytics. Are you receiving such a stream of demand data? If not, do you have a strategy to get it?

Are you holding your marketing and commercial operations to the same standards as your supply chain?

Supply-chain metrics have matured to the point where most sources of variation are understood and acted on in real time at every touch point along the chain. It helps that all of this information is measured in dollars and cents and is generated from a perfectly balanced accounting system. It also helps that the impact of poor performance is visible to all . . . empty shelves or stacks of inventory. Accountability is crystal clear.

In contrast, demand-chain metrics are far less mature, far less precise, and exhibit a far wider range of variation due to the untested collection systems, lack of data standards across the Internet, and most important, changing customer and consumer demands. Accountability is less clear . . . often completely neglected. In this new demand-driven economy, the winning companies will cast a wider and wider network of demand-driven metrics: They will ask their teams to stay in relentless pursuit of the unexplained variation; they will prosecute consumer-driven variation (latent demand!) with the full power and alignment of the supply chain; and they will demand accountability.

Another important characteristic of supply chain management is cycle time. The benefits of cycle-time reductions are clear to all: customer responsiveness, forecasting precision, and obsolescence all improve. Intellectual inventory is no different. In fact, the benefits can be even greater. As opportunities in the demand chain are researched and uncovered, the speed with which new products are brought to satisfy these demands bring untold riches. What cycle-time metrics are in place to reinforce this discipline?

We all know demand metrics will never approach the precision of accounting. What we lose in precision, we will gain in judgment. Winners will be unafraid to exercise informed judgment every step of the way.

Are you merely selling to your consumers?

Marketing is now about enlisting consumers into the community of the product or service. You have to change your relationship with consumers, from selling to them to working with them.

The classic modern example of this is Apple. Its army of millions of rabid customers is its true marketing arm: they provide most of its publicity, organize its sales, and provide creative ideas for its advertising. With the iPhone, Apple provided the platform and the tools . . . and thousands of designers created hundreds of thousands of application programs for the device, many of them for free. These same folks were already working on programs for the iPad when it was still just a rumor on the Web.

How much participation do *your* consumers have in the design, manufacture, packaging, delivery, and service of your products or services? And since that participation also creates a powerful feedback loop to greater understanding of the need states of those consumers, are you even looking for—much less capturing—that information?

Is your media spending aligned to reach precisely the right consumers?

Do you know which specific TV programs, radio shows, magazines, and Web sites will appeal to your most important customers? Digital and other technologies allow for increased precision and timely measurement on the effectiveness of advertising and merchandising strategies. There is enough information today, and new models for purchasing media so that you can get to a more precise target. Within two to three years, you will be able to make much more precise media purchases to create greater value by having a more precise match between your media and the consumers you want. The system is good today, but it will be even better tomorrow.

MEETING YOUR DESTINY

We wrote this book for smart companies—and if you are reading this, you are no doubt part of one. We hope that in these pages we have not only convinced you of the need to prepare yourself for a demand-driven economy, but opened your eyes to the amazing number of programs and tools already available to help you compete in this new world. Many of them are tried and true, but others—which we are showing to the world for the first time—are proprietary techniques we have developed over the last twenty years in real-life practice with some of the world's biggest companies.

These tools work, as the case studies show, and they can be applied *right now.* Evolving from a supply-driven company to a demand-driven company is as much a matter of attitude as it is a process. If your thesis for winning is revised to include the critical challenge of finding your high-profit demand pools and then giving them what they want; if your orientation shifts from asking what your best customers want now to what they want *next;* and if your company's mental model re-aligns your organization away from making your supply chain a little more perfect to making it a lot more accurate, then these are not going to be the worst of times, but the best of times. Your company will enjoy bigger profits, greater market share, and higher customer loyalty, even as your competitors struggle and fade. And it all begins with a change of perspective.

Business is always about change. And each new era reshuffles the deck to come up with a new list of winners and losers. In this book we've shown you how companies will win in the new demand-driven economy. What you do with that knowledge is up to you. The bad news is that you can no longer say you didn't see the change coming. The good news is that your destiny is now in your hands.

NOTES

Introduction

1. http://www.search.com/reference/Disintermediation, accessed March 5, 2010.
2. http://www.instantshift.com/2010/03/26/the-history-of-online-shopping-in-nutshell/, accessed March 7, 2010.
3. http://www.informationweek.com/news/Internet/webdev/showArticle.jhtml?articleID=193000623, accessed April 8, 2010.
4. Erich Luening, "IE leads Navigator in Corporate Browsing," *CNET News*, May 18, 1999, (http://news.cnet.com/IE-leads-Navigator-in-corporate-browsing/2100-1023 _3-225995.html, accessed May 25, 2010); "Zona Research Browser Study Reveals Significant Shift in Primary Browser Usage in the Enterprise; 62% of Enterprises with Corporate Browser Policies Choose Microsoft IE," *Business Wire*, May 18, 1999, (http://www.thefreelibrary.com/Zona+Research+Browser+Study+Reveals+Significant+Shift+in+Primary . . . -a054653357, accessed May 25, 2010).
5. "Microsoft's Internet Explorer Global Market Share Is 95% According to One Stat.com," *M2 Presswire*, December 16, 2002, (http://www.highbeam.com/doc/1G1-95489550.html, accessed May 25, 2010).
6. http://www.google.com/corporate/history.html, accessed April 8, 2010.
7. http://investor.google.com/fin_data.html, accessed April 8, 2010.
8. "His Mission: Simplify Podcasting," *BusinessWeek*, May 24, 2005; http://en.wikipedia.org/wiki/Odeo, accessed April 8, 2010.
9. Andrew Lennon, "A Conversation with Twitter Co-Founder Jack Dorsey," *The Daily Anchor*, February 12, 2009, (http://www.thedailyanchor.com/2009/02/12/a-conversation-with-twitter-co-founder-jack-dorsey/); Claudine Beaumont, "The Team Behind Twitter: Jack Dorsey, Biz Stone and Evan Williams," Telegraph.co.uk, November 25, 2008, (http://www.telegraph.co.uk/technology/3520024/The-team-behind-Twitter-Jack-Dorsey-Biz-Stone-and-Evan-Williams.html, accessed May 25, 2010).
10. http://en.wikipedia.org/wiki/Twitter, accessed April 8, 2010; analysis based on Claudine Beaumont, "Twitter Users Send 50 Million Tweets per Day,"

Telegraph.co.uk, February 23, 2010, (http://www.telegraph.co.uk/technology/
twitter/7297541/Twitter-users-send-50-million-tweets-per-day.html, accessed
May 25, 2010); Debbie Turner, "Twitter General Election 2010: Measuring Opinion by Tweets," *Online Social Media*, April 7, 2010 (http://www.onlinesocialme
dia.net/20100407/twitter-general-election–2010-measuring-opinion-by-tweets/).

Chapter 1: The Demand-Driven Company

1. McDonald's corporate Web site (http://www.aboutmcdonalds.com/mcd/our_
company/mcd_history.html?DCSext.destination=http://www.aboutmcdonalds
.com/mcd/our_company/mcd_history.html, accessed May 25, 2010); http://
en.wikipedia.org/wiki/McDonald's, accessed May 25, 2010.
2. McDonald's Annual Report, 2000.
3. "Big Mac's Makeover—McDonald's Turned Around," *The Economist*, October 16,
2004.
4. Janet Adamy, "How Jim Skinner Flipped McDonald's," *The Wall Street Journal*,
January 5, 2007.
5. Andrew Martin, "The Happiest Meal: Hot Profits," *The New York Times*, January
11, 2009; Interview with Jim Skinner, February 23, 2010.
6. Conor Cunneen, "McDonald's Turnaround Offers Crucial Lessons for All Opera-
tors," *Nation's Restaurant News*, February 18, 2008; McDonald's Annual Reports,
1996 to 2000.
7. J. P. Donlon, "McCEO," *Chief Executive*, June 2009.
8. Scott Hume, "Counter Attack; McDonald's CEO Jim Skinner's Relentless Focus
on Improving Customers' Dining Experiences Has Revitalized the World's Largest Foodservice Brand," *Restaurants & Institutions*, December 1, 2007.
9. McDonalds Annual Report, 2003; Skinner interview.
10. Martin, "The Happiest Meal"; Skinner interview.
11. Skinner interview.
12. McDonald's Annual Report 2009; McDonalds' Annual Report 2004; Scott
Hume, "The 2005 R&I Top 400 Chains Display Leadership and Muscle," *Restaurants & Institutions*, July 1, 2005; "Top 400 Chain Restaurants of 2009," *Restaurants & Institutions*, July 9, 2009; Max Olson, "The McDonald's Success Story,"
FutureBlind, October 26, 2009.
13. Ibid.
14. Ibid.
15. Ibid.
16. Martin, "The Happiest Meal."
17. "Sitting Pretty," *Chicago Tribune*, September 14, 2008.
18. Skinner interview.
19. Skinner interview.
20. Quantitative analysis performed by the TCG Economic Center on factors related
to supply-and-demand and trade globalization using data from the following
sources: U.S. Census Bureau, including Statistical Abstracts of the United States
for data from 1950 through 2007; Bureau of Labor Statistics; Bureau of Economic
Analysis: National Income and Items Accounts (NIPA) for data on US GDP;
University of Pennsylvania (http://pwt.econ.upenn.edu/php_site/pwt63/pwt63
_form.php).

Chapter 2: The Demand-Driven Economy

1. Quantitative analysis performed by the TCG Economic Center on factors related to supply and demand and trade globalization using data from the following sources: U.S. Census Bureau, including Statistical Abstracts of the United States for data from 1950 through 2007; Bureau of Labor Statistics; Bureau of Economic Analysis: National Income and Items Accounts (NIPA) for data on US GDP; University of Pennsylvania (http://pwt.econ.upenn.edu/php_site/pwt63/pwt63 _form.php).
2. Ibid.
3. http://www.boozallen.com/consulting-services/supply-chain-logistics, accessed May 25, 2010; http://www.boozallen.com/about/history/history-1980s, accessed May 25, 2010.
4. Ibid.
5. Ibid.
6. Ibid.
7. Bureau of Labor Statistics, (http://www.bls.gov/bls/unemployment.htm, accessed May 25, 2010).
8. Federal Housing Finance Agency data via www.economagic.com; S&P/Case-Shiller home price indices (http://www.standardandpoors.com/indices/sp-case-shiller-home-price-indices/en/us/?indexId=spusa-cashpidff—p-us——, accessed May 26, 2010).
9. National Small Business Association; "Credit crunch freezes hiring, expansion," *CNNMoney.com*, September 25, 2008, (http://money.cnn.com/2008/09/24/smallbusiness/small_biz_credit_freeze.smb/index.htm, accessed May 25, 2010); "Small Businesses Buckling Under Recession's Credit Freeze," *PBS Newshour*, December 14, 2009, (http://www.pbs.org/newshour/bb/business/july-dec09/small-business_12-14.html, accessed May 25, 2010).
10. U.S. Credit Card Reform Act of 2009, (http://www.govtrack.us/congress/bill.xpd?bill=s111-392, accessed May 25, 2010).
11. Bureau of Economic Analysis, National Economic Accounts. Calculated as nominal personal consumption expenditure 2009 = $10, 089.1 billion/ Nominal gross domestic product in 2009 = $14, 256.3 billion; ratio is 70.8%. (http://www.bea.gov/national/nipaweb/SelectTable.asp, accessed May 25, 2010).
12. Bureau of Economic Analysis, Personal Income and Its Disposition: Personal Saving as a Percentage of Disposable Personal Income, (http://www.bea.gov/national/nipaweb/TableView.asp?SelectedTable=58&Freq=Ann&FirstYear=1947&LastYear=2010, accessed May 25, 2010).
13. "From Ozzie to Ricky," *The Economist*, October 3, 2009.
14. Quantitative analysis performed by the TCG Economic Center on factors related to supply and demand and trade globalization using data from the following sources: U.S. Census Bureau, including Statistical Abstracts of the United States for data from 1950 through 2007; Bureau of Labor Statistics; Bureau of Economic Analysis: National Income and Items Accounts (NIPA) for data on US GDP; University of Pennsylvania (http://pwt.econ.upenn.edu/php_site/pwt63/pwt63 _form.php).
15. Adam Smith, *An Inquiry into the Nature and Causes of the Wealth of Nations* (Amherst, NY: Prometheus Books, 1991).

16. Joel Wisner, Keah-Choon Tan, and G. Keong Leong, *Principles of Supply Chain Management* (Mason, OH: South-Western Cengage Learning, 2009).
17. W. Edwards Deming, *Out of Crisis* (Cambridge, MA: The MIT Press, 2000); http://www.referenceforbusiness.com/management/Pr-Sa/Quality-and-Total-Quality-Management.html, accessed April 8, 2010.
18. IMF World Economic Outlook Database, April 2010 (http://www.imf.org/external/pubs/ft/weo/2010/01/weodata/index.aspx, accessed May 25, 2010).
19. Bureau of Labor Statistics, Percentage Change from previous quarter at annual rate in output per hour within non-farm business (http://data.bls.gov:8080/PDQ/outside.jsp?survey=pr, accessed May 25, 2010).
20. Tom Hayes, *Jump Point: How Network Culture is Revolutionizing Business* (New York: McGraw-Hill, 2008).
21. Ken Auletta, *Googled: The End of the World As We Know It* (New York: Penguin Press, 2009).
22. Quantitative analysis performed by the TCG Economic Center on factors related to supply and demand and trade globalization using data from the following sources: U.S. Census Bureau, including Statistical Abstracts of the United States for data from 1950 through 2007; Bureau of Labor Statistics; Bureau of Economic Analysis: National Income and Items Accounts (NIPA) for data on US GDP; University of Pennsylvania (http://pwt.econ.upenn.edu/php_site/pwt63/pwt63_form.php).
23. http://www.businessdictionary.com/definition/Moore-s-law.html, accessed March 5, 2010.
24. http://www.businessdictionary.com/definition/Metcalfe-s-Law.html, accessed March 5, 2010.
25. Thomas Friedman, *The World Is Flat* (New York: Farrar, Straus and Giroux, 2005).
26. Rick Kash, "The Demand Economy and Demand Strategy: Factbase, Issues and Solutions," speech at the Association of National Advertisers, October 12, 2002.

Chapter 3: Demand Profit Pools

1. The Cambridge Group output from project work.
2. The Hershey Company, Business Update Call, June 17, 2008 (http://seekingalpha.com/article/82178-the-hershey-company-business-update-call-transcript?page=2, accessed March 5, 2010).
3. Ibid.
4. The Cambridge Group output from Hershey's project work.
5. The Hershey Company Quarterly Reports, 2009; The Hershey Company Quarterly Reports, 2008.
6. Eddie Yoon, "Tap into Your Super-Consumers," *Harvard Business Review Blog*, November 25, 2009, (http://blogs.hbr.org/cs/2009/11/surprising_insights_from_super.html?utm_content=Google+Reader, accessed May 25, 2010).
7. Best Buy Annual Report, 2009.
8. Ibid.
9. Rajiv Lal, Irina Tarsis, and Carin-Isabel Knoop, "Best Buy Co., Inc.: Customer-Centricity," *Harvard Business Review*, April 18, 2006.
10. "Best Buy Accelerates Journey to Customer Centricity," Best Buy Press Release, May 3, 2004 (http://communications.bestbuy.com/pressroom/includes/releases/May3newsrelease.pdf, accessed April 8, 2010).

11. Interview with Barry Judge, March 12, 2010.
12. The Cambridge Group output from Best Buy project work.
13. http://www.brainyquote.com/quotes/quotes/r/ronaldreag134622.html, accessed March 5, 2010.
14. The Cambridge Group output from Best Buy project work.
15. Ibid.
16. Ibid.
17. Rick Kash, *The New Law of Demand and Supply* (New York: Doubleday, 2001); Conversation with Phil Marineau.
18. Martin Moylan, "Best Buy CEO Brad Anderson to Retire," *Minnesota Public Radio*, January 21, 2009, (http://minnesota.publicradio.org/display/web/2009/01/21/best_buy/, accessed May 25, 2010).
19. Miguel Bustillo, "Best Buy to Target 15% Cellphone Share," *The Wall Street Journal*, June 25, 2009.
20. Judge interview.
21. Best Buy Quarterly Reports, 2009 and 2010.
22. "Best Buy Offers Rosy Outlook for Year. Brisk Sales of Computers Lift Results Even as Margins Are Pressured by Lower-Priced Netbooks, TVs," *The Wall Street Journal*, March 26, 2010.

Chapter 4: The Fifth P

1. http://www.hoovers.com/company/Harrahs_Entertainment_Inc/ryxjri–1.html, accessed March 5, 2010.
2. Gary Loveman: Executive Profile and Biography ((http://investing.businessweek.com/businessweek/research/stocks/people/person.asp?personId=298182&ticker=HET:CN, accessed March 5, 2010); Harrah's Entertainment Investor Relations: Management Team Profiles (http://investor.harrahs.com/phoenix.zhtml?c=84772&p=irol-aboutusManageBio&ID=143793, accessed May 25, 2010).
3. Sudhir H. Kale and Peter Klugsberger, "Reaping Rewards; Customer Relationship Management Efforts and Tough Management Decisions Transformed Harrah's from a Struggling Casino Operator into a Very Profitable One," *Marketing Management*, July 2007/August 2007.
4. Ibid.
5. Ibid.
6. Ibid.
7. Michael Bush, "Why Harrah's Loyalty Effort is Industry's Gold Standard; Casino Owner Rewarded with $6.4B In Revenue; Program Set to Go Mobile," *Advertising Age*, October 5, 2009.
8. Joan Voight, "Total Rewards Pays Off for Harrah's," brandweek.com, September 17, 2007 (http://www.brandweek.com/bw/esearch/article_display.jsp?vnu_content_id=1003641351, accessed May 25, 2010).
9. SAS Case Study (http://www.sas.com/success/harrahs.html), accessed March 5, 2010.
10. Ibid.
11. Bush, "Why Harrah's Loyalty Effort."
12. http://www.sas.com/success/harrahs.html, accessed March 5, 2010.

13. http://www.boozallen.com/media/file/Global_Innovation_1000 _2007.pdf, accessed March 5, 2010.

14. http://adage.com/century/people006.html, accessed March 5, 2010.

15. 2008 Store Systems Study, produced by RIS News and research partner IHL Group (http://www.risnews.com/ME2/Sites/dirmod.asp?sid=&nm=&type= news&mod=News&mid=9A02E3B96F2A415ABC72CB5F516B4C10&tier=3&nid =6EAA70DC2E55476FA1B58199EC26792D&SiteID=358F592F9E1D45D89012D FB60EA03AD3, accessed May 25, 2010).

16. Quantitative analysis performed by the TCG Economic Center on factors related to supply and demand and trade globalization using data from the following sources: U.S. Census Bureau, including Statistical Abstracts of the United States for data from 1950 through 2007; Bureau of Labor Statistics; Bureau of Economic Analysis: National Income and Items Accounts (NIPA) for data on US GDP; University of Pennsylvania (http://pwt.econ.upenn.edu/php_site/pwt63/ pwt63_form.php).

17. Coca-Cola Company, Investor and Analyst Conference Call, November 16, 2009; Ratna Bhushan & Shailesh Dobhal, "Spray-and-pray gone, precision is the real thing," *The Economic Times,* October 12, 2009.

18. Seth Mendelson, "Front & Center," *Grocery Headquarters,* March 1, 2010 (http://groceryheadquarters.com/articles/2010-03-01/Front-and-center, accessed May 25, 2010); "SKU Rationalization Reshapes Retail Shelves," *Retail News* (retailwire.com), July 6, 2009 (www.retailwire.com/discussions/sngl_ discussion.cfm/13848, accessed May 25, 2010).

19. http://www.ballparkfranks.com/about-ball-park-history, accessed March 7, 2010.

20. "Company News: Sara Lee to Acquire Hanson's Hygrade," *The New York Times,* February 9, 1989.

21. Analysis based on Information Resources, Inc. (IRI) sales and volume data.

22. Ibid.; National Hot Dog & Sausage Council (http://www.hot-dog.org/ht/d/ sp/i/38579/pid/38579), accessed March 5, 2010.

23. Elaine Wong, "How Sara Lee's Ball Park Brand Became the Top Dog," *Brandweek,* March 28, 2010 (http://www.brandweek.com/bw/content_display/news-and-features/packaged-goods/e3ie9fc421daf51cf82eb948c8051a9db27, accessed May 25, 2010).

24. The Cambridge Group output from Ball Park project work.

25. Personal conversations with Chuck Hemmingway, Former Director of Marketing, Ball Park, Summer 2009.

26. Sara Lee Meets the Management Analyst Day, September 16, 2009 (http://phx .corporate-ir.net/External.File?item=UGFyZW50SUQ9MjQwODgoNXxDaGlsZ ElEPTM1MTU4NHxUeXBlPTI=&t=1, accessed March 7, 2010).

27. Analysis based on IRI data.

28. The Cambridge Group output from Ball Park project work.

29. Personal conversation with Mike Clabby, Sara Lee Food Scientist, Spring 2008.

30. The Cambridge Group project work, analysis with Nielsen Homescan data.

31. Personal conversations with Steve Clapp, Former VP Marketing Ball Park and Carl Gerlach, Former Director of Marketing, Ball Park, Spring 2008.

32. Analysis based on IRI data; Meeting the Management Analyst Day.

33. Ibid.

Chapter 5: Total Innovation

1. http://www.anheuser-busch.com/History.html, accessed April 9, 2010.
2. Business meeting with August Busch IV.
3. Ibid.
4. Ibid.
5. http://www.boozallen.com/media/file/Global_Innovation_1000 _2007.pdf, accessed March 5, 2010.
6. http://www.brainyquote.com/quotes/authors/t/thomas_a_edison.html, accessed March 5, 2010.
7. Personal conversation with Peter Klein, Fall 2005.
8. Jim Kilts, *Doing What Matters* (New York: Crown Publishing, 2007); conversation with Kilts.
9. Gillette Quarterly and Annual Reports, 2002 to 2005; The Gillette Company Conference Call, March 16, 2004 (http://google.brand.edgar-online.com/ EFX_dll/EDGARpro.dll?FetchFilingHTML1?ID=3547166&SessionID=CuR1 HFq_OCdAl_7, accessed May 25, 2010).
10. Clayton Christensen and Michael Raynor, *The Innovator's Solution* (Boston: Harvard Business School Press, 2003).
11. Richard Boulton, Barry Libert, and Steve Samek, *Cracking the Value Code: How Successful Businesses Are Creating Wealth in the New Economy* (New York: HarperBusiness, 2000).
12. Thomas Stewart, "Accounting Gets Radical. The Green-Eyeshade Gang Isn't Measuring What Really Matters to Investors. Some Far-Out Thinkers Plan to Change That," *Fortune*, April 16, 2001 (http://money.cnn.com/magazines/ fortune/fortune_archive/2001/04/16/301042/index.htm, accessed April 22, 2010).
13. Bronwyn Hall, Adam Jaffe, and Manuel Trajtenberg, "Market Value and Patent Citations," *Rand Journal of Economics*, 2005, v36 (1, Spring), 16-38.
14. The Cambridge Group output from Sears project work.
15. http://www.starbucks.com/about-us/our-heritage, accessed March 5, 2010.
16. Interview with Tom Wilson, March 3, 2010.
17. Ibid.
18. Ibid.
19. The Cambridge Group output from Allstate project work.
20. Allstate Annual Report, 2004.
21. Personal conversation with Ed Biemer, Winter 2004.
22. Wilson interview.
23. Ibid.
24. Ibid.
25. http://www.regis.com/about/, accessed March 5, 2010.

Chapter 6: The Price Is Right

1. "The Power of Pricing," *The McKinsey Quarterly*, Number 1, 2003.
2. Ibid.
3. Quantitative analysis performed by the TCG Economic Center on factors related to supply and demand and trade globalization using data from the following sources: U.S. Census Bureau, including Statistical Abstracts of the United States for data from 1950 through 2007; Bureau of Labor Statistics; Bureau of Economic

Analysis: National Income and Items Accounts (NIPA) for data on US GDP; University of Pennsylvania (http://pwt.econ.upenn.edu/php_site/pwt63/pwt63_form.php).

4. Rafi Mohammed, *The Art of Pricing: How to Find the Hidden Profits to Grow Your Business* (New York, NY: Crown Business, 2005).
5. http://www.grocerynetwork.com/progressivegrocer/profitguides/beer/v2/news/article_display.jsp?vnu_content_id=1003939944, accessed March 5, 2010.
6. Young & Rubicam, Brand Asset Valuator, 2003.
7. Adam Smith, *An Inquiry into the Nature and Causes of the Wealth of Nations* (Amherst, NY: Prometheus Books, 1991).
8. Fortune Brands Annual Report, 2002. Sales declined from 2000 to 2001 . . . back up in 2002, so 2003 annual report shows increase.
9. The Cambridge Group output from Swingline project work.
10. Ibid.
11. Swingline market share data; Wendy Cole, "The Stapler Wars," *Time*, March 6, 2005.
12. Swingline sales data; The Cambridge Group output from Swingline project work.
13. The Cambridge Group output from a range of consulting project work.
14. The Cambridge Group output from project work for major pharmaceutical company.
15. Ibid.

Chapter 7: Organizing to Win

1. Personal conversation with Ed Liddy, Winter 2010.
2. Allstate Insurance Annual Report, 1998.
3. Allstate Insurance Annual Report, 2007.
4. Liddy conversation.
5. http://joemontanabiography.com/, accessed March 5, 2010.
6. http://finance.yahoo.com/q/is?s=HPQ&annual, accessed March 5, 2010; HP Annual Report, 2009.
7. http://www.hp.com/hpinfo/abouthp/histnfacts/museum/earlyinstruments/0002/index.html, accessed March 5, 2010.
8. David Packard, *The HP Way: How Bill Hewlett and I Built Our Company* (New York: HarperBusiness, 1995); HP Corporate Objectives, 1957 to 1990.
9. HP Annual Report, 1990.
10. HP Annual Report, 2009.
11. Motorola Annual Reports, 1999 to 2000, 2004 to 2008.
12. http://www.apple.com/pr/library/2005/jun/06intel.html, accessed March 5, 2010.
13. Rick Kash, "The New Law of Demand and Supply," speech at Motorola, Inc., November 11, 2003.
14. http://mediacenter.motorola.com/content/detail.aspx?ReleaseID=12263&NewsAreaID=2, accessed March 5, 2010.
15. Interview with J. P. Bilbrey, conducted by Rick Kash and Jason Green on March 12, 2010.
16. Ibid.
17. http://www.thehersheycompany.com/about/; accessed March 5, 2010.
18. The Hershey Company Annual Report, 2008.

19. Bilbrey interview.
20. Andrew Ross Sorkin; "Mars to Buy Wrigley for $23 Billion," *The New York Times*, April 28, 2008.
21. Michael J. de la Merced and Chris V. Nicholson, "Kraft to Acquire Cadbury in Deal Worth $19 Billion," *The New York Times*, January 19, 2010.
22. Bilbrey interview.
23. The Cambridge Group output from Hershey's project work.
24. Bilbrey interview.
25. Ibid.
26. Ibid.
27. Ibid.
28. The Hershey Company Q4 2009 Earnings Call, February 2, 2010; Annual Report 2009; Annual Report 2004.
29. Ibid.
30. Bilbrey interview.

Chapter 8: The Demand Chain
1. Bureau of Economic Analysis; National Economic Accounts.
2. Adam Smith, *An Inquiry into the Nature and Causes of the Wealth of Nations* (Amherst, NY: Prometheus Books, 1991).
3. Interview with J. P. Bilbrey, conducted by Rick Kash and Jason Green on March 12, 2010.
4. http://en-us.nielsen.com/main/measurement/data_fusion, accessed March 5, 2010.
5. Bilbrey interview.
6. Ibid.

Chapter 9: Supply, Meet Demand
1. Personal conversation with CEO of large consumer goods manufacturer.
2. http://royal.pingdom.com/2008/09/24/why-is-almost-half-of-google-in-beta/, accessed March 5, 2010; Paul McNamara; "Almost Half of Google Products—Including 4-Year-Old Gmail—Remain in Beta: Why?," *NetworkWorld*, September 24, 2008 (http://www.networkworld.com/community/node/33131).
3. http://www.apple.com/pr/library/2007/01/09iphone.html, accessed March 5, 2010.

Afterword: A Fresh Start
1. "A-B Earmarks $35M for Bud Light Lime," *Brandweek*, February 12, 2008, (http://www.brandweek.com/bw/esearch/article_display.jsp?vnu_content_id=1003710023, accessed May 25, 2010); The Cambridge Group insights for Anheuser-Busch.
2. Rick Kash, *The New Law of Demand and Supply* (New York: Doubleday, 2001), 191-201.
3. http://www.facebook.com/pampers?v=app_295649897299#!/pampers?v=wall, accessed March 5, 2010.
4. http://www.kraftrecipes.com/home.aspx, accessed March 5, 2010.

INDEX